EDITOR: MARTIN WINDROW

OSPREY MILITARY MEN-AT-ARMS SERIES 260

# PETER THE GREAT'S ARMY 1: INFANTRY

*Text by*
ANGUS KONSTAM
*Colour plates by*
DAVID RICKMAN

Published in 1993 by
Osprey Publishing Ltd
Michelin House, 81 Fulham Road, London SW3 6RB


ISBN 1 85532 315 x

Filmset in Great Britain
Printed through Bookbuilders Ltd, Hong Kong

**Acknowledgements**
The author is indebted to several people for their assistance in his research: his especial thanks to Igor Komarov and Alexei Levokin of the Kremlin Armoury, Yuri Levkin of the State Historic Museum, Moscow, the staff of the Royal Armouries, Francis Turner and Peter Konstam for their translations, Peter Berry and, of course, Anton Alanovitch.

**Editor's Note:**
A full bibliography appears in Peter the Great's Army 2: Cavalry.

# INTRODUCTION

The figure of Tsar Peter the Great dominated Russia in the 18th century. On his accession, the country was an inward-looking feudal state, resistant to change and suspicious of outsiders. Within a few decades his reforms, as well as his policy of increased repression and territorial expansion, had brought about changes from which no section of Russian life remained immune. The policy of 'looking towards the West', which entailed opening up Russia to the Western European countries, paved the way for her emergence as a major European power.

In no area was this more clearly achieved than in the army. Military expenditure dominated the economy, and Russia's increasing resources were harnessed to fulfil military needs. As Christopher Duffy has put it, however, it was inherently easier to hew the forests, to dig, to smelt and fashion the metals than to create a powerful army of reliable troops, led by officers of courage and expertise. Peter's successes and failures in these last respects were to be to a great extent the measure of Russia's military performance in the 18th century.

The French diplomat De Campredon summed this achievement up succinctly in a letter to Louis XV in 1723: 'He has regulated his peoples, making them useful for the service of his state . . . He has worked to drag his nobility up from the subhuman lassitude in which they had sunk, and qualify them to serve in his armies and navies, for which they harboured an invincible aversion until very recently . . . And so, through inconceivable labour and patience, he has managed to form some excellent military and naval officers, a body of splendid soldiers, an army of more than 100,000 regular troops, and a fleet of sixty vessels, including twenty of the line. Russia, whose very name was scarcely known, has now become the object of attention of the greater number of the powers of Europe, who solicit its friendship.'

*Tsar Peter I (1672–1725), First Emperor of all the Russias. The engraving is based upon a portrait painted by Kneller in 1698, when Peter visited England. (Author's collection)*

This military development, impressive in times of peace, took place during a long and bitterly fought war against the Sweden of Charles XII. The Great Northern War (1700–1721) was largely the result of the conflicting territorial ambitions of Russia and Sweden. Russia wanted a trading 'window to the West', and Sweden strove to maintain the Baltic Sea as 'a Swedish lake'. An alliance formed by Russia, Poland-Saxony and Denmark joined forces against Sweden. Their hopes of an easy victory were dashed as Charles XII first knocked the Danes out of the war, then inflicted a disastrous and humiliating defeat on the Russians at Narva (1700). The Russians were saved only by the contempt with which Charles XII viewed them, as he turned his back on Russia and began a lengthy campaign in Poland-Saxony. This six-year respite allowed Peter to rebuild and reorganise his army. Minor campaigns in the Eastern Baltic were used to season his troops.

By the time Charles XII's army invaded Russia in 1708–9, Peter's army was ready for them. Fighting a skilful defensive campaign, the Russians forced the Swedes away from Moscow, and by the spring of 1709 were ready to face the Swedes in battle. At Poltava (1709) Peter won a crushing victory, destroying the Swedish army and forcing Charles XII into temporary exile. The remaining Swedish garrisons in Finland and the Southern Baltic were gradually overrun by the Russians and their re-emergent allies, so that by 1716 the Swedes were reduced to defending their homeland. Charles XII tried to revitalise his country's defences and ailing economy, and defended Sweden from invasion until his death in 1719. The war-weary Swedes, now subjected to Russian raids on the Swedish coast, sued for peace in 1721.

By this treaty Russia supplanted Sweden as the dominant power in the Baltic, and became a major European power. Peter deservedly accepted the titles of 'the Great' and 'Emperor of all the Russias'. On his death in 1725, the man who greeted the birth of his son with the exclamation 'another recruit' had forged a Russian military power that would remain a dominating influence on European military and political thinking until the present day.

***Representation of a Streltsi musketeer of the late 17th century. Note the bardische, which could serve both as a weapon and a musket rest. The curled powder flask is depicted in several near-contemporary illustrations of the Streltsi. Engraving by Jean Baptiste Le Prince, 1768. (Author's collection)***

# CHRONOLOGY

### The Great Northern War

**1700**

| | |
|---|---|
| Apr. | Danish invasion of Schleswig (Sweden's ally). |
| June | Polish-Saxon invasion of Swedish Livonia. Augustus II of Poland besieges Riga. |
| 25 June | Swedish invasion of Zealand by Charles XII threatens Copenhagen. Danes sue for peace. |
| 18 Aug. | Treaty of Travendal. Danes drop out of war. Russians invade Swedish Livonia with 40,000 men. |
| 4 Oct. | Tsar Peter I besieges Narva. |
| 6 Oct. | Charles XII lands in Pernau with 10,000 men. |
| 26 Oct. | Swedes advance on Narva. |
| 17 Nov. | Skirmish at Pyhajoggi Pass, Cossacks retreat. |
| 18 Nov. | Tsar Peter returns to Moscow. |
| 20 Nov. | *Battle of Narva.* Russians decisively defeated; remainder flee back over border. |

**1701**

17 June — Charles XII marches to relieve Riga.

8 July — *Battle of Riga*. Polish-Saxon-Russian force of 28,000 under General Steinau defeated by 18,000 Swedes under Charles XII after Swedes perform assault river crossing of the Dvina. Riga relieved.

9 July — Investment of Dunamunde fortress in Livonia.

Aug. — Swedes invade and annex Courland. Russians raid Swedish Livonia with 8,000 men.

16 Sept. — Skirmish at Sagnitz. Russian raid repulsed.

Oct. — Charles XII enters winter quarters in Courland.

Dec. — Dunamunde capitulates.

**1702**

2 Jan. — Russian General Sheremetev invades Livonia with 12,000 men.

9 Jan. — *Battle of Erestfer*. Swedish army of 7,000 under General Shlippenbach defeated.

Mar. — Charles XII advances on Warsaw.

14 May — Warsaw occupied by Swedes.

19 May — *Battle of Kliszow*. 13,000 Swedes defeat 28,000 Poles-Saxons north of Cracow.

29 July — *Battle of Hummelshof*. Sheremetev defeats remains of Shlippenbach's Swedish army.

31 July — Swedes storm Cracow.

Aug. — Swedish Livonia ravaged by Cossacks.

Oct. — Peter I campaigns in the Neva valley.

21 Oct. — Russians capture Swedish Noteborg fortress guarding Neva River.

| | |
|---|---|
| Nov. | Mouth of Neva cleared of Swedish troops. Russia gains access to the Baltic. |

**1703**

| | |
|---|---|
| Mar. | Charles XII launches new Polish campaign. |
| 21 Apr. | Skirmish at Pulutsk. Charles XII with 2,000 cavalry routs 3,500 Polish cavalry. |
| May | Charles XII besieges Thorn. |
| 16 May | Peter I founds St. Petersburg on Neva River. |
| 4 Oct. | Thorn capitulates. Swedes enter winter quarters. |

**1704**

| | |
|---|---|
| Apr. | Russians under Peter I invade Swedish Livonia; Narva besieged again. |
| 1 June | Swedes advance on Lemberg in S. Poland. |
| 5 June | Peter I besieges Dorpat. |
| 2 July | Charles XII places Stanislas Leszczynski on Polish throne as rival to Augustus II. |
| 14 July | Dorpat capitulates. |
| 24 July | *Battle of Jacobstadt*. Swedes under Lewanhaupt defeat Lithuanian rebel army and Russian contingent in Lithuania. |
| 27 Aug. | Charles XII assaults Lemberg. |
| 26 Sept. | Narva capitulates. |
| 7 Nov. | *Battle of Punitz*. Charles XII defeats an Allied force near the Saxon border. |

**1705**

| | |
|---|---|
| 14 Jan. | Russian force under Ogilvy besieged by Charles XII at Grodno. |
| May | Ogilvy's force slips away to East. |
| July | Swedes pursue Augustus II around E. Poland. |

*Tsar Peter I and his staff at the siege of Azov, 1696. Note the combination of traditional Russian and late-17th-century Western military dress. The Turkish-held city surrounded by Russian siegeworks is depicted in the background. (Private collection)*

Sept. Augustus II escapes Swedish forces, and seeks sanctuary in Saxony.

**1706**

Jan. Augustus II launches campaign from Saxony to recover Poland. Charles sends Rehnskold with 10,000 men to halt him.

13 Feb. *Battle of Fraustadt*. Rhenskold's Swedes inflict a crushing defeat on the 18,000-strong Saxons and Russian army under Schulenburg.

Aug. Swedes invade Saxony, Saxons sue for peace.

Sept. Russian force under Menshikov enters E. Poland and joins Poles loyal to Augustus II. Swedish force under Mardefelt sent to stop him.

14 Sept. Treaty of Altanstadt. Augustus II abdicates; Saxons and Poles make peace with Sweden; Russia alone remains at war with Sweden.

Oct. Charles XII winters his 20,000 men in Saxony.

19 Oct. *Battle of Kalisz*. Menshikov defeats Mardefelt's Swedes, then garrisons Warsaw.

**1707**

27 Aug. Charles XII begins campaign against Russia; Swedes march east from Saxony with 32,000 men.

Oct. Charles XII bypasses Menshikov's defences along the Vistula River.

Dec. Second line along the Niemen River also bypassed by Swedes. Peter I joins Russian army.

**1708**

22 Jan. Skirmish at Grodno. Peter I almost captured; Russians continue to retreat.

Mar. Swedes advance on Minsk.

Apr. 50,000 Russians gather west of the Dniepr River.

June Swedes resume advance. Lewanhaupt with small army and supply convoy ordered to join Charles XII from Livonia.

3 July *Battle of Holowczyn*. 35,000 Russians under Sheremetiev and Repnin forced out of strong position by Swedish assault. Russian retreat continues, and a scorched earth policy is adopted.

*Depiction of a late-17th-century Russian infantryman on a presentation sword produced in Tula during the early 18th century. The soldier wears a uniform combining Russian and Western features. (State Museums of the Moscow Kremlin)*

Aug. Charles XII crosses Dniepr and advances on Moscow.

31 Aug. Skirmish at Dobroe. Russian attack repulsed.

13 Sept. Swedes reach Tatarsk (on Russian border). Scorched earth policy forces Charles XII to turn south, away from Moscow.

29 Sept. *Battle of Lesnaya*. Peter I with 15,000 men decisively defeats Lewanhaupt's 10,000 reinforcements for Charles XII, and captures Swedish supply train.

Oct. Revolt by Cossacks under Mazeppa gives Sweden an ally in the Ukraine. Charles

*The execution of the Streltsi, 1698. Note the mixture of Western uniforms worn by the Guard regiments and the more traditional Russian dress worn by the musketeers of the 'foreign' regiments of Lefort and Boutyrski. Engraving from Baron Korb's* Diary of an Austrian Secretary, *1863. (Private collection)*

| | |
|---|---|
| | XII forced to march there in search of supplies and winter quarters. |
| Nov. | Menshikov crushes Cossack revolt. |
| 3 Nov. | Swedish army enters the Ukraine. |
| Dec. | Both armies enter winter quarters in Ukraine; worst winter in living memory. |

**1709**

| | |
|---|---|
| 7 Jan. | Costly Swedish assault on Russian garrison at Veprik. |
| Feb. | Swedes resume offensive. |
| 9 Feb. | Cavalry skirmish at Krasnokutsk: Swedish victory. |
| Mar. | Bad weather delays Swedish advance. |
| 2 May | Charles XII besieges Poltava in attempt to bring Peter I to battle. |
| 17 June | Charles XII wounded. |
| 23 June | Peter I's army approach Poltava and construct field defences. |
| 28 June | *Battle of Poltava.* Swedes attacked with 16,000 men, leaving 5,000 to screen Poltava. The attack was disrupted by a series of redoubts supported by cavalry. After a force of 5,000 Swedes under Roos were cut off and destroyed, the remainder of Peter's 40,000 men deployed facing the Swedes. The subsequent Swedish attack was annihilated, and the survivors fled. |
| 1 July | Lewanhaupt and 15,000 Swedes surrender after being trapped against the Dniepr River. Charles XII escapes and seeks asylum in Turkey. |

# THE RUSSIAN ARMY IN THE 1690s

Faced with threats from the Swedes and Poles to the north and the Turks to the south, the Muscovite state needed a large army to defend its interests. Unfortunately, the army inherited by Peter was a slothful and badly led mass, incapable of performing its duties adequately.

When Peter won control of Russia in 1689 the army available to him consisted of noble cavalry, irregular Cossack cavalry, the Streltsi, and 'foreign' style foot regiments of dubious quality. The returns of that year list 80,000 regular foot and 32,000 cavalry (both noble and Cossack). This force, the army of Prince Golitsyn, was ignominiously defeated by the Crimean Tartars. In 1716 Peter I wrote that 'the army proved incapable of standing not just against civilised nations, but even against barbarians'.

## The Streltsi

The nearest Russia had to a standing army in the 1690s were the 'Streltsi' (musketeers). Founded in 1550, this 45,000-strong corps was grouped into 22 Regiments, 16 of which were based in Moscow, with three each in Novgorod and Pskov. They regarded themselves almost as a 'praetorian' élite, but by the late 17th century their military commitment was often deemed less important than their ancillary civilian trades, and involvement in Kremlin intrigues. While their peacetime duties included fire-fighting and the enforcement of law and order, their wartime performance failed to live up to the expectations of the Tsar.

Both officers and men were native Russians, resistant to religious and political change, which brought them into conflict with Peter I and his programme of reforms. Following the Streltsi revolt (1698) the Moscow regiments were disbanded and the provincial regiments gradually amalgamated into Peter's new army. These provided a stiffening of experienced troops amongst the new levies. The six Pskov and Novgorod Streltsi regiments participated in the Narva campaign.

The Streltsi were dressed in the traditional Russian long coat (*kaftan*) in regimental colours, with matching fur-trimmed hats. Their normal armament was either a pike, or both a matchlock musket and a bardiche (used as a musket rest). The pike-to-musket ratio was approximately 1:3.

*Sergei Bukhvostov (1659–1728), 'the first Russian soldier' and early* poteshnyi. *He is dressed in the uniform of a major of artillery (c. 1720–5). Painted by an unknown contemporary artist. (The Russian Museum, St. Petersburg)*

## 'Foreign' Regiments

Although Tsar Alexis (Peter's father) had raised a force of 80,000 conscripted infantry organised in the 'foreign' style, only two regiments existed in 1695: those of Francis Lefort (First Moscow) and Patrick Gordon (Boutyrsk). The other 61 regiments were disbanded between 1689 and 1695. It was recorded that this horde of conscripts lacked any military discipline: 'They have neither stomach for great things, nor do they achieve them' (Korb).

## Irregular Infantry

Peter I occasionally made use of irregular foot during the 1690s. 120,000 conscript militia were raised for the Azov campaign of 1695, partly from disbanded 'foreign' regiments. This militia was also partly mobilised during the Streltsi revolt (1698). Of little military value, they have been described as 'a mob of the lowest and most uncouth ragamuffins' (Korb). These troops appear to have had no issued uniform,

*Russian troops at the siege of Azov, 1696. This highly inaccurate portrayal not only includes regular Dragoons, who were not formed until 1701; the Guard infantry also wear the post-1720 pattern uniform. Note the stylised depiction of the Turkish defenders. Watercolour from Krekshnin's* History of Tsar Peter I. *(The Lenin Library, Moscow)*

and so probably wore the traditional *kaftan* and fur-trimmed hat.

Dismounted Cossacks were also employed during the assault on Azov (1696), where their performance was praised by foreign observers.

### The 'Poteshnyi'

In 1682, the ten-year-old Tsar Peter and his mother moved to the royal lodge at Preobrazhenskoe, away from the dangers of the Kremlin. Once there he gradually formed a miniature army, ostensibly to teach himself the military arts. The original '*Poteshnyi*' (from *poteshna*—amusement) were fellow children as well as servants and retainers. The first to join was a 25-year-old groom, Sergei Bukhvostov, recorded in 1683 as 'the first Russian soldier'. (He died in 1728 as a Major of Artillery.) Military equipment, powder, and supplies were provided from the Kremlin Arsenal, including two artillery pieces. These 'play soldiers' were first organised as a 100-strong company of Bombardiers, which later became a title of honour in the new army; Peter himself was enrolled as 'the First Bombardier'. (The original Bombardiers later became a form of military 'inner circle' who, when deemed experienced enough, were given proper military commands.) The *poteshnyi* regularly fought wargames near Preobrazhenskoe, and as Peter became older their numbers grew.

By 1685 they numbered 300, quartered in specially built barracks near Preobrazhenskoe, and as their ranks increased a similarly sized group was quartered in barracks in the nearby village of Semyonovskoe. By this time Peter had begun to study the art of fortification, so a small fort was built near Preobrazhenskoe, which was bombarded by the growing *poteshnyi* artillery train. As the wargames increased in complexity professional military advice was sought, and foreign officers living in Russia were hired as temporary instructors. These foreigners eventually became the permanent officer corps of the *poteshnyi*, and thus eventually of the Russian army.

Further drafts of Streltsi volunteers in 1687 raised the number of *poteshnyi* to 600, who were then organised into the *Preobrazhenski* and *Semenovski* companies, soon to become the first and second regiments of the Russian Imperial Guard. At this stage, both units included artillery and cavalry attachments.

When the Regent Sophia attempted a coup in 1689, the *poteshnyi*, most of the Streltsi and the leading *Boyars* (nobles) backed Tsar Peter, forcing Sophia into exile. Despite his assumption of political power, he left the running of the country to his mother and her advisors while he continued his military games at Preobrazhenskoe. The only difference was that now there was no limit to the resources he could call upon. The *poteshnyi* wargames con-

*The return of Tsar Peter I to the Kremlin from his 'great embassy' to Western Europe, 25 August 1698. The soldiers are incorrectly shown wearing the post-1720 pattern uniform. Watercolour from Krekshnin's* History of Tsar Peter I. *(The Lenin Library, Moscow)* tinued for a further five years under the supervision of General Patrick Gordon, a Catholic Scot who had served in Russia since 1661.

These increasingly large and complex manoeuvres were also dangerous: the Tsar himself was wounded by a grenade in 1690, and in the following year the boyar Dolgorukov was killed. The largest manoeuvre was staged from September to October 1694 near Koshuchovo, when six regiments of Streltsi and 920 'old troops' including cavalry defended a fortification against the two *poteshnyi* regiments, the regiments of Gordon and Lefort, and a further conscript regiment under a Col. Scharf. In all, 15,000 men were involved in the exercise, which resulted in victory for the *poteshnyi* and a not inconsiderable list of casualties.

The *poteshnyi* had proved their worth, and Tsar Peter was now ready to commit them to battle in earnest.

## The Guard Regiments

The two *poteshnyi* companies were expanded, and officially became the *Preobrazhenski* and *Semenovski* Regiments of the Guard on 25 April 1695. Officially referred to as Life Guard Regiments, these became the first and second regiments respectively of the Russian Guard. The Guard became the Imperial Guard in 1721. This date was carried on the 'Alexandr Nevski' ribbon on their standards throughout their history. Indeed, an early colonel of the Preobrazhenski Regiment was Tsar Peter I himself, and subsequently it became the rule for every Russian monarch until 1917 to hold the title of 'First Colonel' of the regiment. (Peter only accepted this honour in 1704, after holding the rank of Bombardier since 1695.)

They were initially organised into 12 companies, each of approximately 100 men, grouped into three battalions. In addition, from 1697, there was a separate Bombardier Company of the Preobrazhenski Guard, formed principally from the ranks of the original Bombardiers, which was used as a special field artillery (*pushkari*) battery comprising six mortars and four field guns.

This organisation was changed in1700, when the Preobrazhenski Regiment was reorganised into four battalions, and the Semenovski into three. The combined strength of both regiments at the Battle of Narva (1700) was recorded as 2,936 men, with each battalion organised into four companies of 100 men each, excluding officers, senior NCOs and drummers. In the establishment of 1704 a Grenadier Company was added to each regiment, which unlike the Line Grenadiers were never brigaded into combined Grenadier Regiments.

*Fusilier of the Preobrazhenski Guard regiment, 1700–20. An early pattern plug bayonet is being fitted to a 'Baltic-lock' musket. The Fusilier's armament and the depiction of Narva in the background indicate that the soldier is from Peter's first army of 1699–1700. Engraving from Viskovatov's* Rossiskoi Imperatorskoi Armii *(St. Petersburg, 1844–56).*

When the two regiments were officially formed the majority of senior commissions were filled by foreigners, although some officers came from the ranks of the original Bombardiers. The only exception to this was the appointment of members of the

*Pikeman of the Preobrazhenski Guard regiment, 1700–20. Note the ornamental pike head, probably issued only to Guards regiments. The pennon is black with silver tails, and embroidered in gold. Engraving from Viskovatov's* Rossiskoi Imperatorskoi Armii *(St. Petersburg, 1844–56).*

Russian nobility. Although promotion in the Petrine army was based upon merit rather than rank, an exception was made for boyars who already had a degree of military experience. For example, Prince Repnin was appointed Lieutenant-colonel of the Preobrazhenski Guard, and the Boyar Golovin was promoted to General and the Commander of the Guard.

Peter I always saw the role of the Guard as much in political as in military terms. The two regiments were used as a training school for young nobles who, once they proved themselves, could be given a commission, either in the Guards or in a Line regiment. These youngsters would initially join at 16, serving first in the ranks as private soldiers. Russian noblemen officers, having accepted the direction of the Petrine reforms, could then be sent on missions to ensure that the reforms were carried out, be they in the military, administrative or economic fields.

The military career of the Preobrazhenski and Semenovski Guard Regiments reflected their dual political and military role. They both formed the core of Peter's army during the Azov campaigns of 1695 and 1696 against the Turks, which was their first experience of combat. Commanded by General Gordon, they supressed the revolt of the Streltsi in 1698, thus safeguarding the Tsar's political interests. At the Battle of Narva, 1700, they proved the only steady troops on the field, together with Lefort's regiment, and helped stop the Russian rout becoming a massacre. Following Narva they were used as a central reserve stationed in Moscow (and later in St. Petersburg), taking part in only three campaigns. Both regiments were instrumental in the clearing of the Neva valley, in particular the amphibious assault of the Noteborg (Schlusselburg) in 1702. They were also awarded a medal for Peter's first naval action, when guardsmen in small boats captured Swedish vessels anchored in the Neva Delta. They participated in the assault on Narva, 1704; and the guardsmen were also called upon during Charles XII's invasion of Russia, when both regiments participated in the Battle of Poltava, 1709.

# THE NEW MODEL ARMY OF 1700

Following the Streltsi revolt of 1698, the only standing army existing in Russia consisted of the Preobrazhenski and Semenovski Guards, the 'old regiments' of Lefort (First Moscow) and Gordon (Butyrski), and the remaining provincial Streltsi regiments. One of the most important features of Peter's vision for his new state was a modern army, modelled along Western lines.

A proclamation was published in November 1699, calling for volunteers. 'Concerning the enlistment of willing men into service as soldiers. Whoever wants to enlist is to have himself enrolled at Preobrazhenskoe, at the "soldier's hut". Such men will be given 11 roubles per year, and will be engaged as soldiers in the Moscow regiments. When on His Majesty's service, and wherever they may be, they will receive rations of flour, fodder and wine on the same basis as the soldiers of the Preobrazhenski and Semenovski regiments.' This plea for volunteers would result in the release of peasants from their serfdom, and would therefore prove alluring; but in order to raise the number of troops required conscripts as well as volunteers would have to be enrolled. In the same month, the Tsar ordered the conscription of serfs from throughout his empire. Each district of the Orthodox Church was ordered to produce 25 men, and secular landowners owning 30 to 50 farms had to provide 30 to 50 men each. This method of conscription was a throwback to the old feudal system of recruitment, and gave the almost exclusively serf army its character.

By the end of January 1700 the recruits had mustered at Preobrazhenskoe, where the Tsar inspected them, and the men were allocated into regiments. Within three months a training programme was under way, when numbers had been swelled to 32,000 by the influx of conscripts. This mass of troops were divided into 27 foot regiments each of between 953 and 1,322 men. These in turn were formed into three divisions, under the command of General Golovin, General Weide and Prince Repnin. Two mustered at Preobrazhenskoe, while Prince Repnin's Division gathered on the lower Volga.

Training was organised by the largely foreign regimental commanders, based upon the drill laid down in Golovin's '*Voinskie Artikuly*' (Military Articles) of 1700. Organisation of the new levy army was left in the hands of Adam Weide, whose '*Regulations*' of 1698 were partly based upon the Austrian model. Tsar Peter took an active interest in the promulgation of the '*Regulations*', and may even have edited parts of the work. The introductory declaration certainly reflected his meritocratic philosophy: '*Soldier* is defined as everyone who belongs to the army, from the highest general to the lowest man.'

The new system of military ranks introduced corresponded to those in Western armies, and for the first time attempted to induce some form of professionalism into the Russian officer corps. In practice, this did not prevent problems with foreign officers. Apart from the inevitable problems of language and the intrinsic Russian suspicion of outsiders, many of those officers appointed turned out to be adventurers with little experience of, and only a half-hearted interest in, their profession. Many were discharged and replaced on Peter's orders, and the proportion of native Russians in the officer corps was increased, although mainly at fairly junior levels.

This was the army with which Russia entered the Great Northern War: two Guards regiments, 27 Line regiments, two dragoon regiments, and a train of artillery. In addition, the remaining provincial Streltsi regiments and the Cossacks could be called upon to aid the new-modelled army. This hastily prepared force would have to face the battle-hardened Swedish army before the end of the year. 'It is only the veteran soldier who has been broken in by many years of training that is worthy of the glory of real warfare' (Korb): Peter's army had months rather than years in which to train.

The debacle at Narva exposed the shortcomings of the Russian army; in Peter's words: 'There was only one veteran regiment, that of Lefort. The two Guards regiments had been in two attacks on Narva

*Fusiliers of Line infantry regiments, 1700–20. Notice the variety of issued longarms and smallswords. Two of the figures are wearing the* kartuz. *Engraving from Viskovatov's* Rossiskoi Imperatorskoi Armii *(St. Petersburg, 1844–56).*

town, but they had never fought a battle in the open field, let alone against a regular army. In the rest of the regiments, a few Colonels excepted, officers and men alike were the merest recruits.' The Russian distrust of foreigners exhibited itself after the battle, when the survivors blamed their performance on their foreign officers. Several were murdered, while the army commander at Narva, the Duc du Croi, apparently escaped only by surrendering to the Swedes. The Russians still had a long way to go.

### Post-Narva reforms

Following Narva the Tsar was faced with the task of rebuilding his army. The 23,000 survivors together with the 10,000 men of Prince Repnin's Division gave him the basis from which to work. As Duffy has put it: 'The defeat certainly had the negative advantage of clearing the ground for rebuilding on new foundations.' Fortunately for Peter, Charles XII turned his back on the Russians and began his six-year campaign in Poland, thus giving the Tsar the respite he needed. Over the next few years Peter's policy was to husband and retrain his troops. He was, however, bound by his alliance with Augustus of Poland. Thus in 1701, and again from 1704 to 1706, a Russian division was lent to the Polish-Saxon army, and participated in the string of Allied defeats. Despite these setbacks, this was a period of improvement in fighting experience and morale.

Minor campaigns in Livonia and Ingria (1701–4) produced several small victories which helped the army regain its confidence. After Hummelsdorf (1702), Peter wrote: 'At long last we have beaten the Swedes with superior strength. In a few years we may defeat them when our strengths are equal.' This 'equal' victory at Kalisz (1706) marked a turning point in the army's self-image. The army expanded rapidly between 1701 and 1704, so that by 1705 the establishment stood at: two regiments of Guards, 47 regiments of Line infantry, five regiments of Grena-

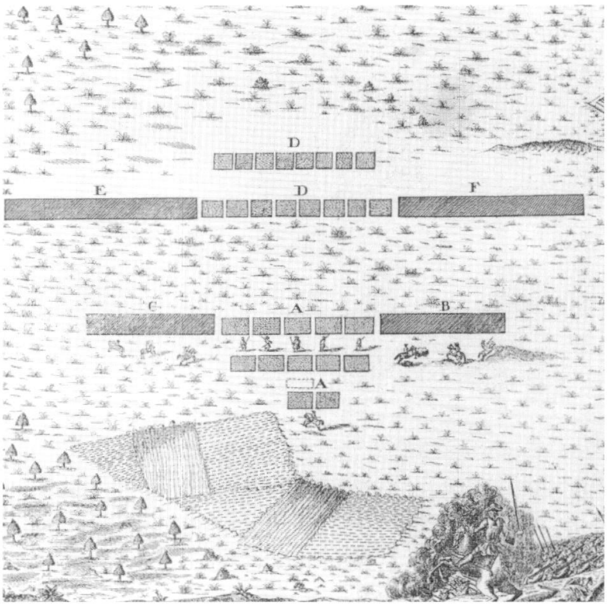

Above *The Battle of Kalisz, 19 October 1706: Russia's first victory over the Swedes with roughly equal forces. (A) Swedish foot; (B, C) Swedish horse; (D) Russian foot; (E) Russian horse; (F) Polish horse. Engraving by Zubov from* The Book of Mars, *1713. (State Historic Museum, Moscow)*

*Capture of the Swedish fortress of Noteborg, 21 October 1702; the fortress guarded the eastern end of the River Neva. The amphibious assault by the Guard regiments was supported by a prolonged artillery bombardment. Engraving by Zubov from* The Book of Mars, *1713. (State Historic Museum, Moscow)* diers, 33 regiments of Dragoons, and one regiment of Artillery. When Charles XII advanced on Russia in 1707, army expansion slowed as the emphasis changed to replacing losses in existing regiments.

The victory at Poltava (1709) justified Peter's military reforms. The highest praise came from his enemies. When the Tsar proposed a toast to the captured Swedish generals, calling them 'my teachers', Marshal Rehnskold replied: 'the pupils have delivered a good return to their masters'. The reform process continued more gradually after Poltava. Garrison regiments were created, and army administration improved. The final 'Military Code' of 1716 consolidated the process, and remained in use largely unchanged until 1900. By Peter's death in 1725 the last trace of the feudal host he inherited had gone, replaced by a powerful regular army organised on European lines.

*General-Field-Marshal Boris Sheremetev (1652–1719); commander of the army during the Livonian campaigns and of the foot at Poltava, he was one of Peter's ablest generals. He was also instrumental in reforming the army after Narva. (State Historic Museum, Moscow)*

# ORGANISATION

In the past, Tsar Peter I has been credited with the first complete remodelling of the old, semi-feudal Muscovite army. In fact, much of the groundwork for his reforms had been laid by his father, Tsar Alexis Michaelovich, assisted by foreign advisers, the principal being General Alexander Gordon.

The army at the start of the Tartar campaign of 1689 consisted of 63 foreign regiments, 44 Streltsi regiments, 8,000 noble cavalrymen, about 2,000 gunners and engineers, and around 10,000 Cossacks: a total of over 150,000 men. The proportion of cavalry in the army was much lower than that found in Western European armies of the same period.

Although regimental organisations appeared to change according to the whims of each successive senior foreign adviser, a basic structure could be determined for the Russian army of the 1680s–90s. The 'foreign' regiments comprised an average of 1,200 men in eight companies of 150 men each. Each company consisted of both pikemen and musketeers, in the ratio of 1:3. Streltsi regiments were larger, with an establishment of 2,000 men, divided into 10 '*Sotnias*' (companies) of 200 men. The use of pikes in the same ratio as in the foreign regiments was a Western imposition which reflected the lack of cavalry in the army.

The new Petrine army was organised for the most part along conventional Western lines. The organisational impetus for this came from a series of military regulations, often written by foreign officers but edited and sometimes altered by Peter himself. Each new regulation was the result of military experience. In other words, the organisation of the army was directly influenced by military experience acquired during the great Northern War or the Turkish campaign of 1711.

### *Regulations of 1698*

Each infantry regiment (*polk*) consisted of two battalions, each of five companies.

The exceptions to this were the Preobrazhenski Guard regiment, which had four battalions, and the

*General-Field-Marshal M. Golitsyn (1675–1730); as a divisional commander he led the Russian attack at Dobroe (August 1708), and commanded the Guards at Poltava. Portrait by an unknown contemporary artist. (State Historic Museum, Moscow)*

Semenovski Guard regiment and Moscovski, Kievski, Narvski and Ingermanlandski Line regiments, which each consisted of three battalions. Each regiment was commanded by a colonel, almost invariably a foreigner, while a lieutenant-colonel or major commanded the remaining battalion(s). In addition, a battery of two 3-pdr. guns was attached to each regiment. (See Tables A & B.)

*Regulations of 1704*

The new 'establishment' created by General Ogilvy whilst campaigning in Livonia was based on the experiences of the Narva and Neva campaigns. The 'enlarged' regiments retained their extra battalions, and all regiments kept their regimental artillery battery. Each infantry battalion was to consist of four companies of Fusiliers, while in addition each regiment received a further company of Grenadiers. The basic company organisation remained the same, with the addition of two sergeants, two corporals and 31 other ranks (*soldniki*).

*Reforms of 1708*

Although no complete set of military regulations was produced, a number of reforms were introduced. On 10 March 1708 an edict from Peter stated that henceforth regiments would be named after provinces and towns rather than after their colonel. This increased regimental pride and allowed traditions to continue when the colonel changed. From 1708, the Grenadier companies attached to each regiment were split from their parent unit and used to form five 'converged' Grenadier regiments. Only the two Guards regiments and the Ingermanlandski and Astrakhanski Line regiments retained their Grenadier companies.

*Reforms of 1712*

The ukase of 19 February 1712 laid down a new standard regimental establishment of 1,487 men in two battalions, each of four Fusilier companies and an attached battery of two regimental guns. This was broken down as follows: 3 senior officers; 34 junior officers; 32 sergeants; 48 corporals; 16 drummers; 9 musicians; 1,120 soldiers; 29 non-combatants; 24 artisans; 86 drivers; and 86 servants (*denchikii*).

*Code of 1716*

On 30 March 1716 Peter published the 'Military Code of the Year 1716' (*Ustav Voinskoi 1716 goda*), a military manual that remained in use largely unaltered until 1900. Under the new organisation, the Guards regiments and the Ingermanlandski regiment consisted of three battalions, the remaining 35 Line regiments having two battalions. Regimental strength remained largely the same as laid down in the ukase of 1711, apart from the attached *denchikii*, who were reduced from 86 to 54.

All these military organisations reflected the official strength of a unit. Losses from starvation, disease, desertion and, to a lesser extent, from combat would reduce these strengths markedly.

## Army organisation

During the entire reign of Peter the Great there was no permanent military organisation in the Russian

## Organisation of a Two Battalion Russian Regiment, 1700

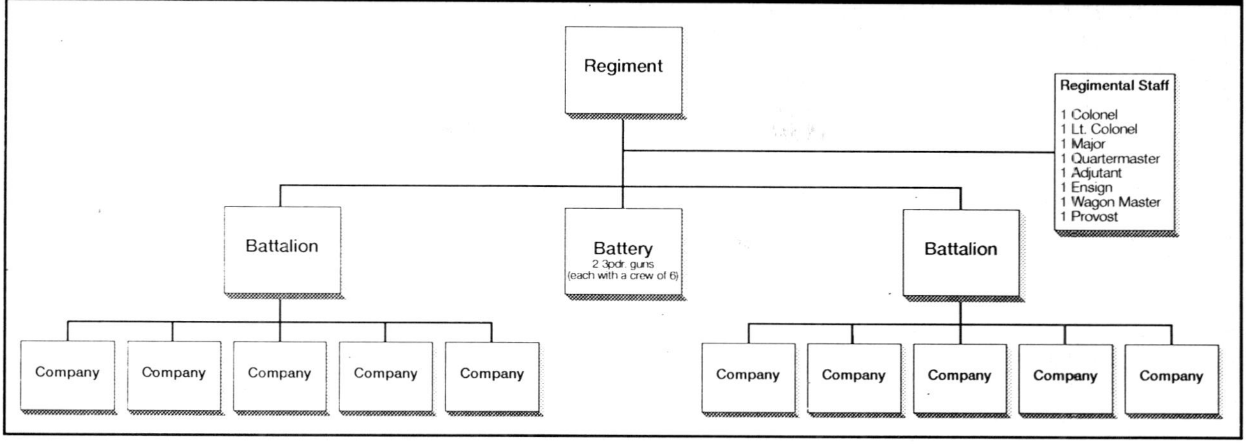


## Strength of a Russian Company, 1700

**Company**

1 Captain
1 Lieutenant
1 Ensign
1 NCO Ensign
1 Captain of Arms (Armourer)
1 Doctor
1 Adjutant
1 Clerk
4 Corporals
2 Drummers
18 Pikemen
84 Fusiliers

army above the regimental level. The army of 1700 was organised into three 'divisions' each of nine regiments, which in turn were sub-divided into three or four 'brigades' of two or three regiments each. This reflected the situation which existed in the majority of contemporary Western armies.

The Code of 1716 also emphasised that higher formations could be formed and reformed during a campaign. The 'division' was defined as 'an army formation, in which several brigades come together under the direction of a single general'. In peacetime it was also used as an administrative formation for a number of regiments billeted in the same province. The 'brigade' was simply defined as a formation which comprised two, three or more regiments. This allowed the composition of *ad hoc* formations, such as the special force commanded by Peter at the Battle of Lesnaya in 1708. In the Code of 1716, it was described as: 'a *korvolan* (flying corps) ... of between six and seven thousand men. ... For these purposes we employ not only the cavalry, but also the infantry, armed with light guns, according to the circumstances of time and place'.

# RECRUITMENT & MANPOWER

### The officers

The majority of the officers appointed to Peter's first army were foreigners, principally Saxons. These proved of variable quality, the best available officers no doubt already serving in the Saxon army of Augustus II. The English ambassador in Russia, Charles Whitworth, wrote in January 1707: 'they have a great want of experienced officers ... the most they have are Saxon men of little reputation, and it is a question whether they will keep their companies and not fall into some gross disorder on the approach of the enemy'. General Manstein, writing of his military observations during Peter's reign, describes these foreign officers as being 'the most useless throw-outs from the rest of Europe'.

For this reason the Tsar attempted to increase the number of native Russian officers in the army, largely but not exclusively recruited from the ranks of the nobility. The autocratic nature of Peter's Russia was such that the social system could be modified to serve the needs of the state. Thus for the nobility, social status was inextricably linked to state service. Nobles were recruited into state service at the age of 16, into either the army, navy or the civil service. Connections ensured enrolment as a common soldier into the Guard regiments, whose ranks rapidly became filled with potential officers serving a period in the ranks while gaining knowledge of their profession.

A Petrine edict of 1714 attempted to introduce a programme of military education to increase professionalism. This avoided the situation where young officers were: 'either ignorant of the fundamentals of soldiering, or if they had served in the army, have one so only for show and for a matter of weeks or months' (Beskrovnyi). Other influences were exerted on these potential young officers. Hundreds were sent abroad in 1700 and 1705, and colleges teaching military skills were opened. This led to a steady improvement in the standard of native Russian officers.

Military ranks in the Western style were introduced, and in 1722 the Table of Ranks equated these to similar naval and civil ranks, ensuring a guaranteed level of status and pay. One of the advantages of the Petrine system was the emphasis on promotion by merit, where commoners could be made officers, and thus achieve ennoblement. The ranks used throughout the Petrine period were as follows:

| | |
|---|---|
| *Generalissmus* | (supreme commander) |
| *General Feldmarshal* | (field-marshal) |
| *Generalshef* | (general) |
| *General Poruchik* | (lieutenant-general) |
| *Major-General* | (major-general) |
| *Brigadir* | (brigadier) |
| *Polkovnik* | (colonel) |
| *Major (1st)* | (major 1st class) |
| *Major (2nd)* | (major 2nd class) |
| *Kapitan* | (captain) |
| *Poruchik* | (lieutenant) |
| *Podporuchik* | (2nd lieutenant) |
| *Praporshchik* | (ensign) |

The last four were deemed 'under-officer' ranks, the rest classified as being 'over-officers'. Guard officers were graded two ranks higher than their given rank.

Military rank meant responsibility as well as privilege. The edict of 1716 stated: 'As the officers are

***Full-dress uniform of a colonel of the Preobrazhenski Guard regiment, c. 1720–5. This example belonged to Tsar Peter I. The sash colours are red over blue over white. (State Historic Museum, Moscow)***

*Detail of an engraving of the Battle of Poltava, 28 June 1709, by Nicolas de Larmessin. The Russian regiments on the left are deployed in two lines, the battalions interspersed with regimental guns. (State Hermitage Museum, St. Petersburg)*

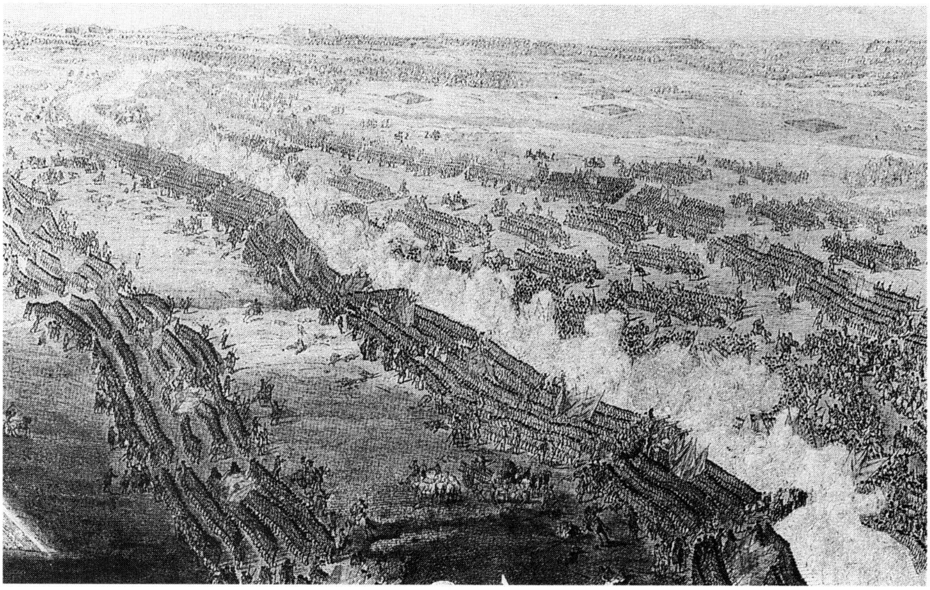

*The Order of St. Andrew, with associated light blue sash. Instituted by Peter I, the order was awarded to senior officers for outstanding achievement on behalf of the state. Recipients included Sheremetev, Menshikov and the tsar himself. (State Museums of the Moscow Kremlin)*

to the soldiers as fathers are to children, so they must act in a paternal fashion and as the children without question obey their fathers, and lay all their hopes with them, they in turn should look after maintenance, instruction, nourishment and all that is required.' This relationship between officers and men was a world removed from that found in Western armies; these paternal responsibilities and increasing professionalism were, of course, embraced more eagerly by some than others. A later 18th-century Western officer noted that: 'There can exist ... striking differences between individual officers of the same regiment' (Masson).

The improvement in the quality and number of native Russian officers was a gradual process but, by 1725, 42 out of 65 officers ranked major-general or above were Russian, as were most under-officers.

### The men

Peter's first army was a mixture of volunteers and conscripts, but after Narva the need for soldiers outweighed any considerations of free will. A national levy in 1701 was followed by a system of compulsory military service in 1705, which continued throughout Peter's reign. Any voluntary scheme of enrolment was abandoned largely because it undermined the tight control of serfs by the Russian landowning classes.

Conscription meant that in theory all classes were obliged to perform military service. In practice,

*Officer of a Line infantry regiment, 1700–32. No standard uniform was issued to commissioned officers. This captain wears a green coat faced red, a sash in the national colours, and a tricorne trimmed with gold feathers. Engraving from Viskovatov's* Rossiskoi Imperatorskoi Armii *(St. Petersburg, 1844–56).*

conscripts were chosen by landowners or village councils, later replaced by district authorities (*voevodas*). Naturally, the least productive members of society were chosen: 'If amongst his peasants or servants there is an incorrigible thief, then he will send him. In the absence of a thief, he will dispatch a drunkard or an idler' (Langeron).

Military service was for life, later reduced to a period of 25 years. The high attrition rate due to sickness, starvation or fatigue meant that most conscripts would never return to their homes. From 1705 to 1715 an average of 40,000 men were conscripted each year, most aged between 16 and 20. Desertion was rife, despite a move in 1712 to brand conscripts, and those who survived long enough to join their regiments found conditions extremely punishing.

Discipline was harsh. The initial disciplinary codes dated from the reign of Tsar Alexis, but Peter revised these in 1716. Both codes were characterised by their severity, and were based on the civilian system of deterrents. The penalty for minor offences was hanging, while more serious capital offences were punished by decapitation, breaking on the wheel, or burning. More minor punishments included piercing the tongue with a red-hot iron, savage beatings with the knout, or, after 1716, the Swedish punishments of sitting on a wooden horse or running the gauntlet. On occasion, units which had been routed were subjected to a lottery which chose one man in ten to be shot, while his colleagues were simply beaten. Although the more serious punishments were severer than those normal in many Western armies of the period, they mirrored the Russian civil codes. A later Russian officer commented: 'Foreign armies are composed of freemen, and ours of serfs. The first kind of person must be treated with some circumspection, whereas our men are long-enduring and docile' (Orlov).

Rations took the form of an issue of flour and water, from which the soldiers baked bread or *sukhare*, a type of biscuit. When available this diet was supplemented by cabbage, used to make *shchi*, and washed down with *kvas*, a weak beer produced from rye bread. Meat, when available, had to be purchased by the soldiers themselves, or the artel—a group of about 25 men messing together.

Training was the responsibility of the individual regiment, based upon the successive Military Codes. Drills for firing and manoeuvring were laid down for the whole army, but it was not until 1716 that a standardised schedule of training was introduced. One of the problems with Peter's army was the lack of suitable NCOs, all being serfs promoted from the ranks. Therefore, in 1721, a soldiers' school was founded in each garrison town, whose aim was to increase the number of NCOs, scribes and artisans in the army.

Although the lot of the Petrine soldier was hard and his chances of survival slim, the stoic attitude and tolerance of appalling conditions resulting from

## Table C: Infantry Regiments 1700–25

| Regiment | Notes |
|---|---|
| *The Guard* | |
| 1. Preobrazhenski | |
| 2. Semenovski | |
| *Line* | |
| *Raised before 1699:* | |
| 1. Lefort | (Lefort) First Moskovski from 1712 |
| 2. Butyrski | (Butyrski) |
| *Raised in 1699:* | |
| 3. Rostovski | (Caspar Golz) |
| 4. Kievski | (Wilhelm von Delden) |
| 5. Sibirienski | (Friedrich von Werden) |
| 6. Vologdski | (Roman Bruce) |
| 7. Pskovski | (Col. Mewes) |
| 8. Schlusselburgski | (Matthias Trieden) |
| 9. Archangelski | (Alex Deydut) |
| 10. Nishegorodski | (Col. Bohlmann) |
| 11. Smolenski | (Elias Bils) |
| 12. Tschernigovski | (Col. von Schweden) |
| 13. Asovski | (Ivan Busch) |
| 14. Vladimirski | (Col. Jungor) |
| 15. Kazanski | (Johann von Delden) |
| 16. Moskvaski | (Col. Ivanitsky) |
| 17. Novgorodski | (Nicklaus Balk) |
| 18. Voronezhski | (Theodor Balk) |
| 19. Luzkski | (Nicklaus von Werden) |
| 20. Yaroslavski | (Johamn Treiden) |
| 21. Permski | (Ivan Angler) |
| 22. Vyatski | (Paul Berner) |
| 23. Tverski | (Col. Dewsin) Disbanded 1712 |
| 24. Byeloserski | (Johann Berner) Garrison Rgt. from 1712 |
| 25. Astrakhanski | (Alexander Gordon) |
| 26. Troizki | (Col. Fliwerk) |
| 27. Inglis | (Johann Culom) Viborgskii from 1712 |
| 28. Destroyed 1707 | (Zacharias Crow) Denis Bils from 1701 |
| 29. Destroyed 1707 | (Peter von Buxhowden) Lewison from 1701 |
| *Raised in 1702–3:* | |
| 30. Ingermanlandski | (Alexandr Menshikov) |
| 31. Narvski | (Col. Schonbeck) |
| 32. Koporieschski | (Col. Skripzyn) |
| 33. Tobolski | (Prince Repnin) |
| 34. Ryazanski | (Col. Lange) |
| 35. Nevski | (Col. Kulikov) Not fully raised until 1706 |
| 36. St. Peterbourgski | (Governor Apraxin) Name changed in 1712 |
| 37. Kargopolski | (Stekalov) Disbanded 1712 |
| 38. Ustiugski | (Col. Oserov) Disbanded 1712 |
| 9. Byelgorodski | (Col. Augustov) |
| 40. Yamburgski | (Col. West) Disbanded 1712 |
| 41. Destroyed 1707 | (Col. Romanovski) Old Streltsi Regt. |
| *Raised in 1704:* | |
| 42. Destroyed 1707 | (Col. Kanischtschev) Old Streltsi Regt. |
| 43. Destroyed 1707 | (Col. Danilov) Old Streltsi Regt. |
| 44. Destroyed 1707 | (Col. Nelidov) Old Streltsi Regt. |
| 45. Destroyed 1707 | (Col. Gulitz) Old Streltsi Regt. |
| 46. Olonetzski | (Col. Scharf) |
| 47. Galitschski | (Col. Stubensk) |
| *Raised in 1706–7:* | |
| 48. Ivangorodski | (Col. Bokan) |
| 49. Rentzel | (Col. Rentzel)[1] |
| *Raised in 1708:* | |
| 50. von Fichtenheim | |
| 51. Schnewenz | |
| 52. Simbirski | |
| 53. Periaslavski | |
| 54. Sotovski | |
| 55. Tolbuchin | |
| 56. Fraser | |
| 57. Ostrovski | |
| 58. Schmidt | |
| *Disbanded in 1712 (used to form the cadres of the Garrison Infantry regiments):* | |
| Kargopolski | |
| Olonetzki | |
| Simbirski | |
| Tverski | |
| Oustioneyski | |
| Yambourgski | |
| Ivangorodski | |
| Pereslavski | |
| Belozerski | |
| *Raised in 1722 (Army of the Lower Caspian) – also known as the* Nizevoi Dorpous[2]*:* | |
| 59. Asterabadski | |
| 60. Bukutski | |
| 61. Hyrkanski | |
| 62. Schirvanski | |
| 63. Sinsiliski | |
| 64. Masenderanski | |
| 65. Derbentski | |
| 66. Ryazhtschki | |
| 67. Daghestanski | |
| *Grenadiers[3]:* | |
| 1. Prince Repnin's | (later Taylor's, then Lacey's) |
| 2. Busch's | (later Weide's, then Hallart's) |
| 3. Ensberg's | (later Du Bois, then Kampenhausen's) |
| 4. Bieltz | (later Hagen's) |
| 5. Prince Baryatinski's | (later Sykov's) |

Note: The name in brackets is the regimental name used before 1708, when, following the Tsar's *ukas*, almost all regiments were named after a town or province. The number given refers to seniority only; no regiment was given a regimental number, as was the case in some Western armies.
(1) Formed from the survivors of the Battle of Fraustadt (Regiments listed as 26–7, 42–5).
(2) Regiments 59–67 were created to guard the new Russian territories acquired during the Caspian campaign. They were formed from existing regiments, as follows: four companies each came from the Grenadier Regiments Sykov and Kampenhausen, and the Line Regiments Luzki, Schlusselburgski, Azovski, Kazanski, Ryazanski, Nishegorodski, Moskovski, St. Petersburgski, Viborgski, Galitishski, Troitzki, Sibirski, Koporyeschski, Archangelski, Pskovski, Voronezski, Tobolski and Vologdski. The Daghestanski Regiment had no Grenadier Company.
(3) The first four composite Grenadier Regiments were formed in 1708, the last-named in 1710 from the Grenadier Companies of Line Regiments. After 1708 only the Guard Regiments and the Ingermanlandski and Astrakhanski Regiments retained their Grenadier Companies.

serfdom enabled him to endure army life. This tendency was reinforced by increasing national pride and a normally fervent Orthodox religious belief. The old Russian soul, even when clothed in a uniform of Western cut, remained the same; when the soldier was freed from his former master he simply moved into a new kind of lifelong serfdom.

Although the serf nature of the army meant that initiative and skilled training were lacking compared with other European armies, the system did have its advantages. Throughout the 18th century Russian soldiers displayed, when adequately led, a level of

## Table D: Regiments at Poltava, 1709

**Foot**

*Guard Regiments*
Preobrazhenski
Semenovski
*Grenadier Regiments*
Bieltz
Busch
Du Bois
Prince Repnin
*Line Regiments*
Apraxin
Azovski
Ingermanlandski
Yaroslavski
Kievski
Lefort
Moskovski
Narvski
Nischin-Novgorodski
Novgorodski
Pskovski
Schlusselburgski
Troitski
Siberienski
Vologdski
von Rentzel
*Garrison Regiments*
Byelgorodski
Natyaevski
Nekludovski

**Horse**

*Cavalry Escort*
The Life squadron
Menshikov's squadron
*Horse Grenadier Regiments*
Kropotov
Roschnev
van der Roop
*Dragoon Regiments*
Archangelski
Azovski
Ingermanlandski
Yaroslavski
Kievski
Moskovski
Narvski
Nevski
Nischnin-Novgorodski
Novgorodski
Novotroitski
Permski
Riazanski
Sibirienski
Tverski
Viatski
Vladimirski
Vologdski

**Artillery**

Total of 72 guns
In redoubts (Augustov):
1 light battery
2 medium batteries
Main train (Bruce):
1 light battery
2 medium batteries
2 heavy batteries
2 mortar batteries

endurance and stoic courage which was unusual in other armies. '... Taken as individuals the Russians are gentle, even timorous. But massed in battalions they manifest a herd-like cohesion which makes them redoubtable, and sometimes unbeatable' (Masson).

*Detail from the 'Battle of Poltava' mosaic by Mikhail Lomonosov, 1756. The Russian soldier despatching the Swede is incorrectly dressed in the post-1720 pattern uniform of the Preobrazhenski Guards. (The Academy of Sciences, St. Petersburg)*

# UNIFORMS & EQUIPMENT

## Uniforms

From their inception Tsar Peter dressed his *poteshnye* in uniforms of a Western cut, completing the Westernisation of dress begun by the 'foreign regiments' of Tsar Alexis. When the new army was formed in the winter of 1699–1700 these Western styles were adopted by the whole army, save elements of the noble or irregular cavalry. With the exception of a few particularly Russian features such as the *kartuz* the army now resembled its Western counterparts, at least in dress. The basic features of the Petrine uniforms were similar for Guard, Grenadier and Line regiments alike, with each regiment having a uniform colour chosen by the regimental commander.

As the Russian textile industry was in its infancy, the majority of material for early Petrine uniforms was imported from England and Holland. The materials used were coarse, and quality varied almost as widely as regimental coat colours. The cost of clothing was deducted from the soldiers' pay.

No dress code was imposed for officers, and they usually wore finer quality versions of the soldiers' coats, embellished with gold trim. This freedom meant that officers' coats need not have been of the same colour as the regiment to which they belonged.

The uniform coat (*kaftan*) was of a 'German cut', knee length with no collar. The sleeves were folded back into substantial cuffs, exposing the lining. Both the cuffs and the button-hole linings were normally of a different colour from the *kaftan*. The pocket flaps were cut with a serrated flap secured by four tin buttons, while a further three buttons held each cuff in place. The *kaftan* was fastened by 13 to 16 plain tin buttons, depending on the length of the coat. In 1720 a new pattern of coat was introduced; this was similar, but with a wide collar and less decorated pockets, secured by three buttons. A cord on the left shoulder helped secure the cartridge box in place.

The coats of regimental musicians (fifers, drummers and oboists) were identical to the normal soldiers' coats with the addition of a 'swallow's nest' or epaulette on the right shoulder. This was of the same colour as the coat and was piped in the national colours (white, blue and red) with lace trim.

A waistcoat (*kamzol*) was worn underneath the *kaftan*; of a similar design, it was shorter, had no cuffs and was of a closer cut. The front was fastened by 18 buttons, while the sleeves and pockets were secured by three and four buttons respectively. The 1720 pattern *kamzol* differed only in the shape of the pockets, reflecting the new *kaftan*. Officers and Guard soldiers' waistcoats were edged with gold trim.

Cloth breeches (*pantaloni*) were worn to just below the knee, and secured at each side by six tin buttons. The front was flapped in the style of sailor's trousers. Woollen stockings (*chulkii*) reached above the knee and were secured by a small black leather strap and buckled garter. Although they were normally worn under the breeches, some illustrations depict soldiers in battle wearing them over the top. Shoes were of a 'German pattern', in stiff black leather with a pronounced tongue, a round brass buckle and square toes. Neckerchiefs were worn by all troops, frequently made from fine black cloth and knotted at the front, the ends left to hang over the vest and shirt. The white linen shirt itself was collarless, with slightly gathered sleeves and a drawstring neck. In 1720 white neckerchiefs were issued, a colour previously only worn by some officers.

Dragoons and pikemen were also issued with buff leather gloves, although supplies appear to have been intermittent, and their issue to the infantry was stopped in 1712. Officers' gloves were of similar material, but often embellished with decoration.

The main badge of rank for an officer was a silken sash (*sharf*) in the national colours (white, blue and red, in various combinations). On occasion other colour combinations were used, such as green, gold or silver. Sashes of senior officers were interleaved with silver and gold threads. All sashes were finished with a gold tassel.

Two types of headgear were worn by the Guard or Line infantry. The first, and most common, was the tricorne hat (*treugolka*) of standard European pattern, made of black felt or moleskin, with a white edging trim for Line troops and a gold trim for officers and the Guard. On occasion, officers' *tregolki* could be further embellished by red and white

*Non-commissioned officers of the Preobrazhenski Guard regiment, 1700–20. Both sergeants carry halberds; one corporal is armed with a 'fusil', while the other carries a regimental banner. Engraving from Viskovatov's* Rossiskoi Imperatorskoi Armii *(St. Petersburg, 1844–56).*

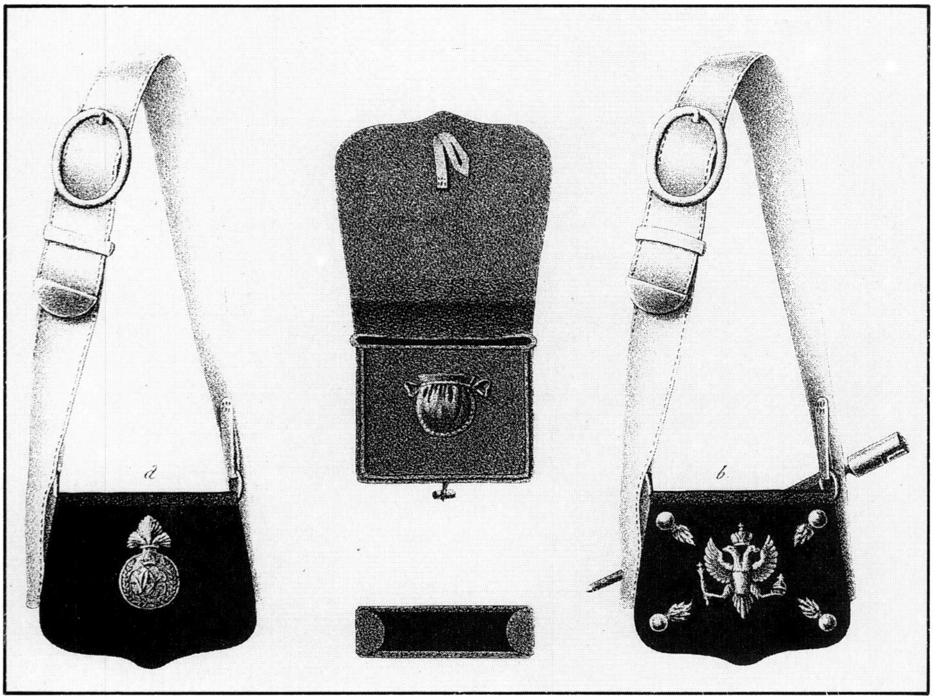

*Cartridge pouches, 1700–20. The left hand example is that of a Line Fusilier, the right hand box being the pattern issued to Grenadiers. Early boxes were unadorned. Those issued to Guard regiments resembled the Grenadier box but omitted the flaming grenade motif. Engraving from Viskovatov's* Rossiskoi Imperatorskoi Armii *(St. Petersburg, 1844–56).*

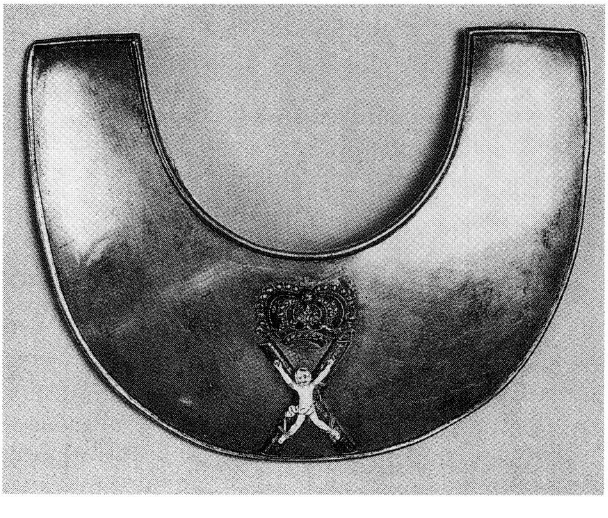

*Officer's gorget c. 1706–20, one of several variants; the decoration is painted onto the brass surface. It was suspended from the neck using crimson ribbons. This example is reputed to have belonged to Tsar Peter I/ (Artillery Museum, St. Petersburg)*

feathers lying inside the turned-up brim. The front left brim was secured by a single brass button. The second type was a cloth bonnet (*kartuz*). This was worn by certain Line infantry and Dragoon regiments instead of the *treugolka*. The lining was frequently of a different colour from the outside, giving it a two-toned appearance. As protection against inclement weather the cap could be pulled down in a similar manner to a modern balaclava.

Grenadiers wore a mitre (*grenaderskaya tshapka*), the Guard version differing from that of the Line. The mitre worn by Line infantry Grenadiers and Horse Grenadiers consisted of a pointed cloth bag, with turned-up flaps at the front or back, trimmed with white piping. The point was surmounted by a gold cord tassel. Guard grenadiers wore a black leather spherical helmet fitted with a neck protector. A brass plate fitted to its front displayed a Russian eagle, while a smaller oval plate at the back carried the monogram of Tsar Peter I. On occasion a red and white striped ostrich plume could be attached to the rear of the helmet.

A greatcoat (*shinel*) completed the issued attire. This ankle-length woollen garment was fitted with a large collar and buttoned cuffs. A second outer collar could be buttoned round the neck as protection from the elements; this was usually made from a red material, although some regiments were issued with grey overcoats, the colour used for those issued to Garrison regiments.

## Equipment

All Fusiliers, Grenadiers and front rank pikemen carried a black leather cartridge box (*patronna sumka*) measuring 20cm by 12cm, suspended from a buff leather bandolier slung over the left shoulder. The bandolier was fitted with brass D-rings to secure the box and a brass buckle. Initially unadorned, in 1708 it was decorated with a brass plate carrying Peter I's

Voronezh, 1696:
1: Streltsi, 1st Moscow Regt.
2. Soldatski, Lefort's Regt.
3: Ukrainian Cossack

A

Narva, 1700:
1: Fusilier, Semenovski Gd. Regt.
2: Drummer, Preobrazhenski Gd. Regt.
3: Pikeman, Preobrazhenski Gd. Regt.

B

Dorpat, 1700:
1: Fusilier, Butyrski Regt.
2: Sgt., Ingermanlandski Regt.
3: Fusilier, Pskovski Regt.
1
2
3


C

Poltava, 1709:
1: Fusilier, Narvski Regt.
2: Praporshchik, Narvski Regt.
3: Line Grenadier, Prince Repnin's Regt.
DAVID RICKMAN
'92
1
2
3

D

Poltava, 1709:
1: Tsar Peter I
2: Grenadier,
Preobrazhenski Gd. Regt.

E

Riga, 1720:
1: Sgt., Riga Garrison Regt.
2: Fusilier, Ukrainian Land Militia
3: Fusilier, Nekludovski Garrison Regt.

F

Derbent, 1722:
1: Grenadier, Kampenhausen's Regt.
2: Fusilier, St. Petersbourgski Regt.
3: Major, Simbirski Regt.

G

H

Colours:
1: Colonel's, Preobrazhenski, c.1701
2: Company, Preobrazhenski, c.1706
3: Colonel's, Semenovski, c1701
4: Company, Semenovski, c.1706
5: Colour pattern, Line regts., 1700-1712
6: Colonel's, Line regts., 1712-25

cypher, which was in turn replaced by a Russian eagle plate in 1720. Cartridge boxes used by Guardsmen and Grenadiers were similar, but decorated with brass flaming grenades in the four corners and a Russian eagle respectively from 1708.

In addition Grenadiers carried a second, smaller black leather box slung from the front of their waistbelts, and decorated with the Tsar's cypher and a flaming grenade. This was known as a *lyadunka*, and was used to hold fuzes and the soldier's grenades (*grenada*). Slowmatch (*fitili*) is depicted as being looped around the waistbelt beside the box.

The waistbelt (*portupeya*) issued to Line infantrymen was made from buff leather, sewn along both edges. Those issued to Guardsmen were similar to those worn by officers, being decorated with gold trimming along both edges. A leather sword or bayonet belt-hanger in two loops was suspended from the left rear side of the *portupeya*. The *portupeya* was fastened using a large oval brass buckle.

The drum carried by regimental musicians was wooden, and a surviving example in the Kremlin Armoury is painted a dark green. Two red central fields on opposite sides of the drum were painted with a design similar to that used on standards, with an armoured hand holding a sword point downward extended from a grey cloud. The red oval field was surrounded by a gold chain. The design on the reverse of the drum portrayed a gold Russian eagle on a red field. White straps served to keep the drum taut, and the upper and lower drum bands were painted red. The drum was secured to the *portupeya* by means of two hooks.

The Russian army uniform was standardised by an edict of February 1720, destroying one of the more colourful aspects of the Petrine army. *Kartuzi* were discontinued and replaced by the *treugolka* for all but Grenadiers. The two Guards regiments received dark green coats with red linings and button-holes; the Preobrazhenski wore red collars and the Semenovski light blue. Both regiments were issued with red breeches and vests, with white stockings and neckerchiefs and dark green overcoats. The uniform for Line regiments was standardised following the Preobrazhenski pattern of a green coat with red collar, cuff linings, button-holes and vest, with white stockings and neckerchief, and a red overcoat and breeches.

These uniform colours remained in use until after the death of Peter the Great.

### Infantry weapons

Before Tsar Peter developed links with the centres of European firearms production, no regulation pattern existed for Russian military weapons. Native Russian production was limited, the main centre being the workshops of the Kremlin Armoury. The majority of mechanisms were matchlocks and 'Baltic-lock' snaphaunces, a mechanism introduced through Russia's Baltic neighbours.

During Peter's tour of Western European countries he examined and purchased a large number of weapons, most notably 15,000 firearms of Dutch or English origin in Amsterdam. Most of the longarms purchased were flintlocks fitted with a 'dog-lock' mechanism, a style which was rapidly copied and produced in the emergent Russian arms factories. Other imported weapons were more modern flintlocks, referred to by the Russians as 'French-locks'. This import of weapons continued throughout the Great Northern War; for example, in 1704 the Russian ambassador Matveyev sent 1,498 guns to the

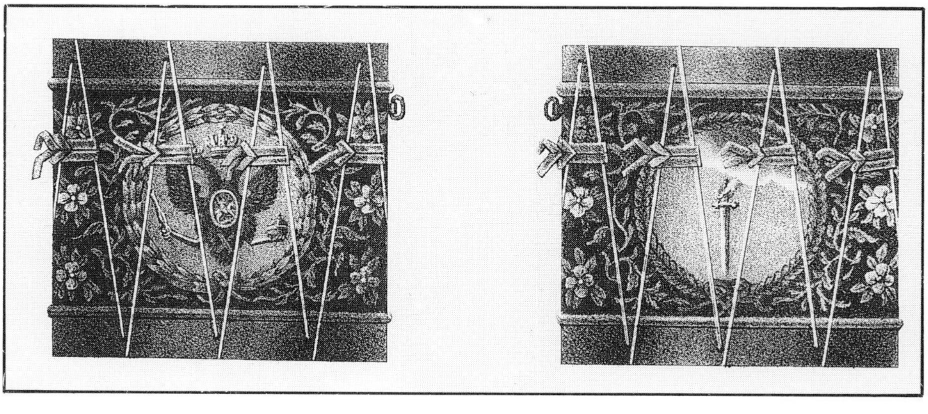

*Infantry drum, 1700–32. Painted black with red banding, the central panels were painted in natural colours on a pale red background. Note the 'D'-ring attachment to hang the drum from the waistbelt. Engraving from Viskovatov's* Rossiskoi Imperatorskoi Armii *(St. Petersburg, 1844–56).*

Kremlin Armoury from Holland, bought from a Dutchman named Klyuk.

By the campaign of 1700 the majority of the army was armed with a variety of imported flintlocks, although earlier Russian weapons were still used. Over the next six years the flintlock appears to have completely replaced the earlier forms of longarms, using a combination of imported and Russian weapons.

As the firearm production centres of Tula, Olonetz, Moscow and St. Petersburg expanded, the production of native Russian weapons increased. Russian factories were capable of producing 6,000 flintlocks in 1701, and by 1706 annual production had

## Table E: Uniform Colours

| Regiment | Headgear | Coat | Breeches |
|---|---|---|---|
| *Guard* | | | |
| Preobrazhenski | Tricorne | Dark green faced red | Dark green |
| Semenovski | Tricorne | Light blue faced red | Light blue |
| *Grenadiers* | | | |
| Prince Repnin's | Red mitre faced blue | Red | Red |
| Weide's | Green mitre with fur band | Green faced red | Red |
| Ensberg's | | | |
| Bieltz's | Blue mitre faced red | Blue faced red | Blue |
| Baryatinski's | | | |
| Line | | | |
| Boutyrski | Yellow kartuz faced red | Red faced green | Red |
| Lefort | Green kartuz faced red | Red faced green | Brown |
| Rostovski | Green kartuz | Dark green faced yellow | Red |
| Kievski | Tricorne | Red faced yellow | Red |
| Sibirienski | Tricorne | Green | |
| Vologdski | White kartuz faced green | Green faced white | |
| Pskovski | Tricorne | Green faced red | Red |
| Schlusselburgski | Red kartuz faced yellow | Green faced red | |
| Archangelski | Tricorne | Dark green faced blue | Red |
| Nishegorodski | Green kartuz faced red | Green faced blue | Brown |
| Smolenski | Tricorne | Dark green faced red | Red |
| Tschernigovski | Tricorne | Red faced blue | Green |
| Azovski | | | |
| Vladimirski | Tricorne | Red faced green | Red |
| Kazanski | Red kartuz faced blue | Blue faced red | |
| Moskovski | Red kartuz faced green | Red faced green | Red |
| Novgorodski | White kartuz faced green | Green faced white | Brown |
| Veronezhski | | Dark green | |
| Luzkski | Blue kartuz | Dark green faced blue | Leather |
| Yaroslavski | | Green | Red |
| Permski | Yellow kartuz faced green | Green | |
| Vyatski | Tricorne | Dark green faced blue | Dark green |
| Tverski | Tricorne | Dark green | Red |
| Byeloserski | | | |
| Astrakhanski | | Green faced red | Brown |
| Troizki | Tricorne | Dark green | Red |
| Inglis | | | |
| Ingermanlandski | Tricorne | Dark green faced red | Brown |
| Narvski | Tricorne | Dark green faced blue | Red |
| Koporieschski | Tricorne | Dark green | |
| Tobolski | Green kartuz faced red | Green | |
| Riazanski | Tricorne | Green faced blue | |
| Nevski | | | |
| Viborgski | | Green | |
| Kargopolski | | | |
| Ustiugski | | | |
| Byelgorodski | Tricorne | Dark green faced red | Brown |
| Yamburgski | | | |
| Olonetzski | | | |
| Galitschski | | | |
| Ivangorodski | Tricorne | Green | Red |
| Rentzel | Green kartuz faced red | Green | |
| von Fichtenheim | | | |
| Schnewenz | Tricorne | Dark green | Brown |
| Ssimbirski | Tricorne | Green | |
| Periaslavski | | | |
| Sotovski | | | |
| Tolbuchin | Tricorne | Red | Red |
| Fraser | Tricorne | Green | Brown |
| Ostrovski | | | |
| Schmidt | Tricorne | Dark green | Brown |

As there was little uniformity, the choice of regimental uniform colours was left to individual regimental commanders; this has resulted in a dearth of available information. The predominant coat colours used were green and red, while grey coats were issued to Garrison infantry regiments. The following information reflects the uniforms worn in 1708–9:

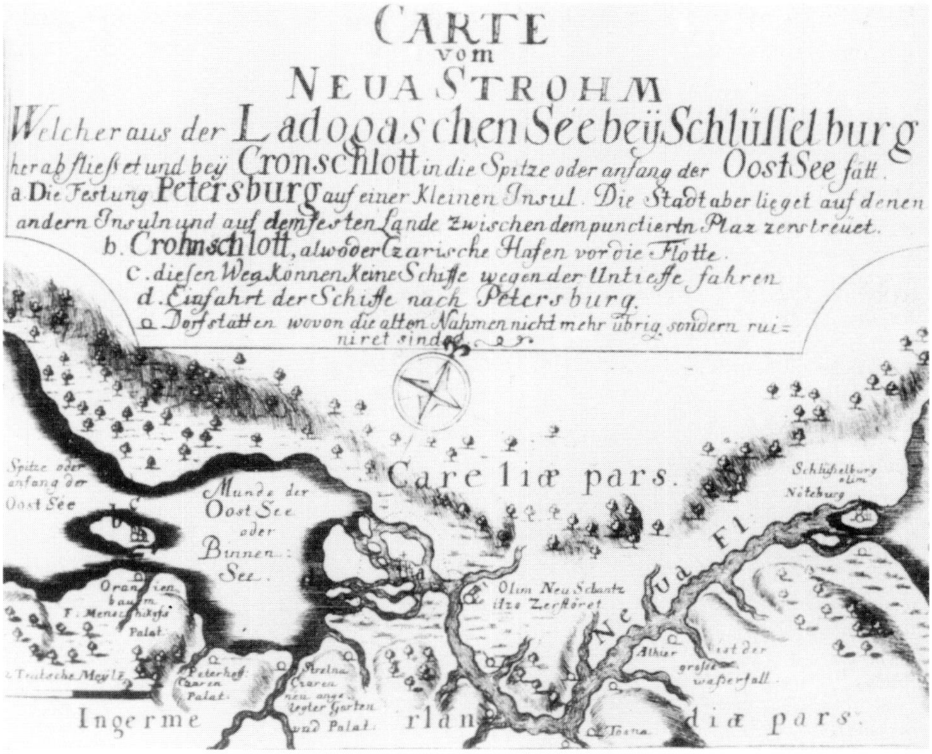


*The River Neva, site of Peter's early campaigns in 1702. Noteborg fortress guarding the eastern end of the Neva was captured in October, followed by the smaller fort of Neuchantz. The city of St. Petersburg was founded in the Neva delta in the following year. The site was guarded by the St. Peter and Paul fortress in the delta, and by the island fortress of Kronslot, in the Gulf of Finland. (Author's collection)*

increased to 30,000 weapons. This was largely due to foreign expertise and the use of modern tooling machines. Despite this, sizes, weights and calibres of longarms continued to vary, so no standardisation could be achieved within any regiment. This lack of standardisation continued throughout the Petrine era, although never to the extent seen in the first few years after Narva. Of the surviving examples, the average flintlock '*fusil*' had a bore of around 16mm and an overall length of about 165cm. These fusils fired an *8 zolotnik* (34g) lead ball with an effective range of 200 metres. The rate of fire of the Petrine army averaged three rounds every two minutes.

No regulation pattern for pistols was introduced until 1735, so a mixture of imported and home-produced weapons were used. Flintlock mechanisms rapidly replaced earlier wheel-locks and 'Baltic-lock' weapons. Pistols were carried by front rank pikemen as well as Dragoons, the latter also being armed with carbines or the heavier musketoon, a weapon resembling a modern shotgun. Sources are unclear whether these musketoons were also used by infantrymen as well as sailors or Dragoons. Their weight may have proved prohibitive, except during a siege. Musketoons with both 'dog-lock' and 'French-lock' mechanism were produced in Russian factories as late as 1716, copied from Dutch originals.

The Petrine infantryman of 1700 was issued with a plug bayonet in lieu of a smallsword. Unlike Western plug bayonets, it resembled the later cutlass bayonet, thus being suited for use as a cutting and thrusting weapon. It fitted into the muzzle of the *fusil* and so prevented any use of the firearm when fitted. This weapon was gradually replaced between 1701 and 1709 by a socket bayonet with a 20cm blade of triangular section, closely resembling its Western counterparts.

Pikemen, officers and Fusiliers issued with a socket bayonet also carried a smallsword. Patterns varied as widely as those of firearms, and imported swords were steadily replaced by weapons of Russian manufacture. Surviving examples display a degree of similarity. The blades have an average length of 90cm, and those produced in Russia appear to have a rapier blade rather than that of a typical smallsword. The blades were surmounted by brass or iron hilts, with wire-bound wooden grips. By 1716 a standard pattern of smallsword had been developed for the use of infantrymen. Officers could carry their own choice of weapon, although set patterns of smallswords were produced in 1716 for Guard and Line officers. All remaining scabbards appear to be of brown or black leather with brass fittings. Officers' sword knots were in the national colours.

Under-officers carried a partizan as a mark of rank. The brass head was engraved with a St. Andrew's Cross or later with a Russian eagle, and was mounted on a 250cm wooden haft, painted black. Sergeants carried an iron-headed halberd engraved with Peter I's cypher and a St. Andrew's Cross. The head was mounted on a similar haft to the partizan. The halberd was frequently used less as a weapon than as an instrument to help dress the ranks.

Each infantry regiment was issued with a number of 340cm pikes. The pike was iron, of a distinctive hollow tripod construction. Examples in the State Historic Museum have an iron socket cast to resemble a lion's head, with the blade protruding from its mouth. These decorated pikes may have been issued to the Guard regiments. Further pikes in the Kremlin Armoury have a simpler three-veined head decorated with a fretwork pattern, and were possibly more typical of Line infantry pikes. All hafts were wooden, painted black.

*Grenadier of a Line regiment, 1700–20. He is depicted wearing a green coat with red facings. The vest, breeches and mitre are also green. Engraving from Viskovatov's* Rossiskoi Imperatorskoi Armii *(St. Petersburg, 1844–56).*

# TACTICS

Before 1701, Peter's Rusian army appeared to have no definitive tactical doctrine, individual foreign commanders being free to adopt their own methods based upon Golovin's *Artikuly* (1700). To a large extent the Austrian method of deploying in six ranks and firing by ranks was adopted as the norm.

Each battalion included 100 pikemen, formed in the centre of the formation in six ranks of 24 files each. As both the Tsar and his army gained military experience pikes seem to have gradually been replaced by firearms in combat. Thus after the Poltova campaign the army would probably have deployed in a manner resembling all Western armies save the Swedes, armed almost exclusively with firearms; but 150 pikes continued to be issued to regiments as late as 1720—along with 3,072 'swine feathers' for use against armies such as the Turks which had a large preponderance of cavalry; on campaign these were carried with the regimental baggage.

In 1708, Peter I issued the 'Rules of Combat' based upon experience gained against the Swedes. (The 'Rules' formed the tactical base of the 'Military Code of 1716'.) The firing formation was reduced to one of four ranks on the Anglo-Dutch model, and the now more experienced troops were trained to fire volleys by ranks or by platoons in the Prussian fashion.

The 'Rules' stated that generally the army would deploy in the Western manner, in two battle lines and a reserve line, with cavalry grouped on the wings. Much was left to the initiative of the army commander, although it was emphasised that 'if it proves necessary, he arranges for the construction of redoubts and entrenchments'. This defensive deployment was a direct result of military experience of Swedish tactics, whose '*ga pa*' offensive doctrine could be countered by the use of firepower combined with fortifications.

The reliance on field fortifications became a dominant Russian military trait, particularly during

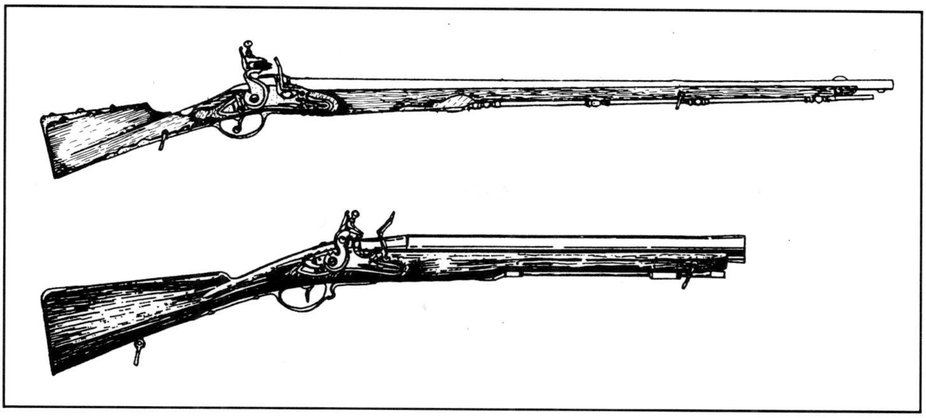

*Russian military longarms, 1700–25. The upper weapon is a 'fusil' fitted with the 'dog-lock' mechanism commonly found on Petrine guns. The lower is a 'musketoon'. (Originals in the State Historic Museum, Moscow)*

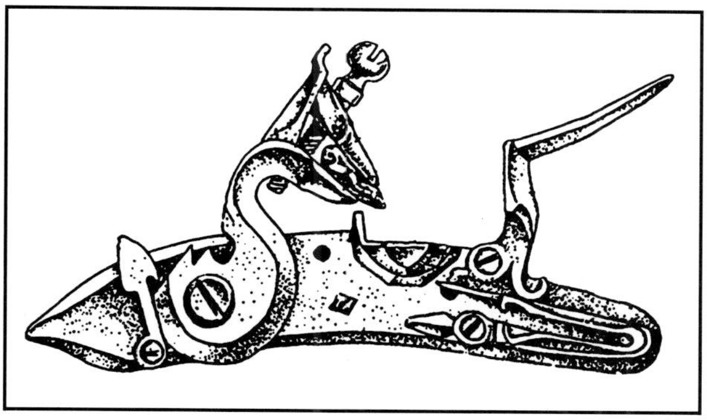

*'Dog-lock' mechanism from a 'fusil' produced in Olonetz in 1708. The 'dog' acted as a safety catch when the gun was cocked. (Original in the State Historic Museum, Moscow)*

the Russian campaign of 1708–9. At Holowczyn, Russian fortifications proved inadequate to the job of halting the Swedish attack, serving only to surrender the initiative to the enemy. At Poltava a new role for fortifications was envisaged where a number of earthen redoubts were used to disorganise the initial Swedish attack, putting the Swedes at a disadvantage during the subsequent phase of the battle. In addition a number of heavily fortified marching camps were built during the Russian advance on Poltava to diminish the risk of a surprise attack, the last of which became a base for operations during the battle.

On the strategic level, apart from the garrisoning of captured fortifications to control newly acquired territories such as Livonia and Finland, less permanent forts were constructed between the Don and the Volga when Azov was returned to the Turks in 1712. Further temporary fortifications were built on river lines in Siberia to protect the conquered territories from Tartar raids.

On the offensive, the use of interdependent but separate columns was advocated (in the manner later used by Napoleon), covered by an advance or flying column of cavalry.

The terrain of Russia or Poland was seen to work to the advantage of the Russians, and could be used to offset the offensive abilities of the Swedes. As Peter wrote to one of his generals: 'I beg you to operate not just in the open field but in woods as well, which can be extremely useful, as I saw myself.'

On an operational and strategic level, the doctrine encapsulating Peter's campaigns during the early 1700s was that of avoidance of battle unless victory was assured. This was principally achieved through concentration of force and therefore local superiority in numbers. The diplomatic requirement to provide a force for the support of the Saxon-Polish army proved a wasteful drain on scarce resources. The other, more successful operations in Livonia and the Neva valley were conducted with superior forces and often under the supervision of the Tsar himself.

The Russian campaign of 1708–9 displayed a visible improvement in operational and strategic planning. Peter proved more able than Charles XII in co-ordinating his secondary armies in support of his main field. A strategy combining substantial field defences for the army behind the north–south river system of Byelorussia was partly successful in channelling the Swedish invasion. When combined with a ruthless scorched earth policy, this proved enough to divert Charles XII from his strategic objective of Moscow.

After Poltava the war entered a largely diplomatic phase during which the Tsar had to curb his desires for territorial expansion and instead provide support for his re-emergent allies. During this time the principal Russian strategy was to extend the territory between St. Petersburg and any enemy into a protective belt reaching as far as the Baltic states and the west of Finland. Garrison regiments held these new territories, allowing the regular army to campaign in support of Russia's allies and to threaten an invasion of Sweden.

During the final years of the war the main Russian striking force was the navy and galley fleet, whose policy of raiding the Swedish coast with forces of regular troops and Cossacks finally forced the Swedes to sue for peace. This military and diplomatic achievement caused some degree of concern in Western Europe:

'The Russians ... grow in their knowledge and experience of military and international affairs, and actually surpass many other nations in slyness and dissimulation' (von Bulow, 1725).

# GARRISON & MILITIA REGIMENTS

### Garrison Regiments

Peter I found that the requirement to use Line regiments to garrison captured territory and to police Russian provinces proved a drain on the field army. His response was to raise Garrison regiments to guard the frontier and to keep internal peace. The ukase of 19 February 1712 ordered the formation of 39 Garrison regiments of 1,483 men each, which were to be named after garrison towns, provinces or, in some cases, after their commanders. Troops from 16 Line infantry and four Dragoon regiments were used as the cadre of these garrison formations. This brought the numeric strength of the army in 1712 to:

62,454 Infantry and Guard (with 10,080 draught horses)
43,825 Dragoons (on 42,900 horses)
64,769 Garrison troops

This made the total strength of the army 171,231 men, excluding gunners.

A number of older units were included in this figure as Garrison troops. Policing troops raised by Tsar Michael Fedorovich in Kazan and Bielgorod had already been used as border guards, as had a number of Streltsi regiments, including the Viborgski, which had become a regular Line regiment in 1704. In addition to these infantry regiments, the Garrison Dragoon regiments of Voronezhski and Kazanski were also raised, as well as the Roslavlski Garrison Dragoon squadron.

Eleven of these regiments garrisoned St. Petersburg, ten were split between Riga, Reval and Pernau, ten in Azov and Kiev (including the cavalry regiments), two in Finland, and the remainder (including the Dragoon squadron) were stationed in Moscow, Smolensk, Archangel, Kazan and Siberia.

By 1716 the number of Garrison units had increased to 49 regiments and one battalion of infantry, and four regiments and one squadron of Dragoons. The garrisoned province was now responsible for contributions to the upkeep of its regiments. These were distributed as follows:

St. Petersburg: 4 regiments
Kronstadt & Kronslot: 2 regiments
Viborg: 3 regiments
Schlusselburg & Kexholm: 1 regiment
Narva: 1 regiment
Reval: 4 regiments
Riga: 4 regiments
Dunamunde: 1 regiment
Pernau: 1 regiment
Moscow district: 2 regiments, 1 dragoon squadron
Kazan district: 3 regiments, 1 dragoon regiment
Azov district: 5 regiments, 1 dragoon regiment
Kiev district: 5 regiments
Siberia district: 3 regiments, 1 dragoon regiment
Archangel district: 2 regiments
Astrakhan district: 1 regiment, 1 dragoon regiment
Smolensk province: 2 regiments
Gluchov: 2 regiments
Veliki Luki: 1 battalion

Garrison formations in the first nine locations were designated 'Baltic' regiments and received higher pay from the other regiments, which were designated 'Internal'. Of the latter, the regiments in the Azov and Kiev districts were regarded as being of lower standing than all other Garrison regiments.

In 1716 the strength for each regiment was given

as 1,319 men in two battalions of four companies each (1,309 men in 'internal' regiments). Dragoon regiments stood at 1,077 men in ten companies, while the Dragoon squadron mustered 544 men in five companies.

The Garrison infantry regiments were dressed as the Line regiments but without vests; instead they wore collarless working coats without lapels, in a coarse grey cloth. The Garrison Dragoon regiments were issued with the same rough working coat but of dark green cloth with red facings and red breeches. All other equipment for both infantry and Dragoons was identical to that issued to Line regiments.

The Byelgorodski, Natyaevski and Nekludovski Garrison infantry regiments (all pre-1712 units) were present at Poltava, where they wore grey coats. There is no evidence to support the legend that Tsar Peter dressed his Guard regiments in grey coats before the battle to give the Swedes the impression that they were only Garrison formations.

### Militia

The problems of garrisoning the Ukraine against Tartar raids and any Cossack revolt resulted in the creation of militia troops separate from the newly created Garrison regiments. The backbone of these formations consisted of militia troops from units raised in the late 17th century by Tsar Alexis Mikhailovitch. These old formations had been charged with guarding the frontier from Kiev to Azov. On 2 February 1713 these were converted into six Ukrainian Land Militia regiments, totalling 9,150 men, with each regiment formed into ten companies. The troops differed from the regular army in that they were all *odnodvortzii* (yeomen), as were the majority of non-Cossack Ukrainians. Peter later converted their status to that of 'crown peasants', charging them 40 kopeks for the privilege. The Ukrainian *odnodvortzii* were also made responsible for maintenance and recruitment of the Land Militia regiments.

*Ukrainian Land Militia Regiments*
Karamsin
Lvov
Kigitz
Ivanenko
Dumin
Bunin

*Guard Grenadier, 1720–5. Woodcut by unknown contemporary artist. The cartoon depiction illustrates the basic uniform features, including the decorated 'helmet' mitre. The grenadier is in the 'present arms' position. (Private collection)*

# INFANTRY STANDARDS

While regiments of the army before 1700 were issued with standards which reflected the feudal and orthodox nature of Russian society, those of Peter's new-modelled army followed the pattern set by Western European countries. Older units, such as Streltsi regiments and traditional cavalry formations, still retained the older pattern of standards. Although the new pattern flags were introduced in time for the Narva campaign, the many surviving examples now held in Stockholm display a remarkable degree of variation upon the basic design. These early standards are well illustrated in Petrelli and Legrelius, *Narvastrofeer* (Stockholm 1907). During the reorganisation of the army after Narva a standard flag pattern was introduced, which remained unchanged until 1712.

The issue of standards remained the same throughout the Petrine era. Each regiment was issued one regimental (or colonel's) colour, and one colour per company. Both types were mounted on a black pole topped by a brass spear-shaped finial. The finial was decorated by two 1-*arshin* long gold tassels. Both standards carried the same design, although the colours of the various elements were not laid down and so could vary.

A gold chain in the centre of the standard enclosed an armoured arm holding a sword point downward. The arm extended from a grey cloud covering the upper portion of the chain. A light rose-coloured circle suspended from the bottom of the chain formed the background to a blue St. Andrew's Cross. The gold chain and cross were in turn surrounded by crossed palm fronds tied together at the base by a ribbon. The colour of the fronds varied, wine red being the most common. On the company colours of both Guard and Line regiments the company number was represented by silver six-pointed stars, one per company. These were located above the chain and between the upper arms of the palm fronds. The background colour of the company standards, where known, was as follows:

*Red* Schlusselburgski, Astrakhanski, Kievski, Azovski.
*Green* Archangelski, Vladimirski, Nevski, Ingermanlandski, Viborgski, Permski, St. Petersbourgski, Kazanski, Sibirski, Tobolski, Suzdalski, Boutyrski, Koporieschski, Troitzki,
*Tawny* Belozerski, Novgorodski, Pskovski.
*Light Blue* Nishegorodski, Voronezhski, Yaroslavski, Narvski, Loutski.
*Blue* Vologodski, Viatski, Moskovski, Riazanski, Smolenski.
*Yellow* Rostovski, Tchernigovski.

The main difference between infantry and dragoon standards was that those of dragoon regiments were fringed with gold thread. On occasion dragoon company standards replaced the central gold chain motif with a cross, a device used on the dragoon standards captured at Narva.

Part of the Petrine military reforms after Poltava included a reorganisation of standards. The ukase of 25 October 1711 outlined the new pattern, which was issued in 1712. The 1712 colours consisted of two separate patterns of standards. The colonel's colour consisted of Tsar Peter I's cypher in gold surrounded by gold palm fronds intertwined with silver flowers and tied by a gold ribbon. The company colour followed no set design, each regiment having a device particular to its assigned town or province in the upper staff corner of the flag, while the remainder of the standard consisted either of a plain field or some form of geometric pattern. Both infantry and dragoon regiments bearing the same regimental name carried standards of the same design.

Throughout the Petrine era army both infantry and dragoon regiments for the most part carried flags of a similar size and design. The 1700–12 pattern measured $2\frac{3}{5}$ *arshins* wide by $2\frac{4}{5}$ *arshins* high. The post-1712 pattern standards were larger, measuring $3\frac{2}{5}$ *arshins* wide by 3 *arshins* high. (One Russian *arshin* = 0.76 metre.)

*Punishment in Petrine Russia was frequently administered with the knout (whip) by both military and civilian authorities. The beating could be of such severity that the offender's back would be broken. Engraving by Jean Baptiste Le Prince, 1768. (Author's collection)*

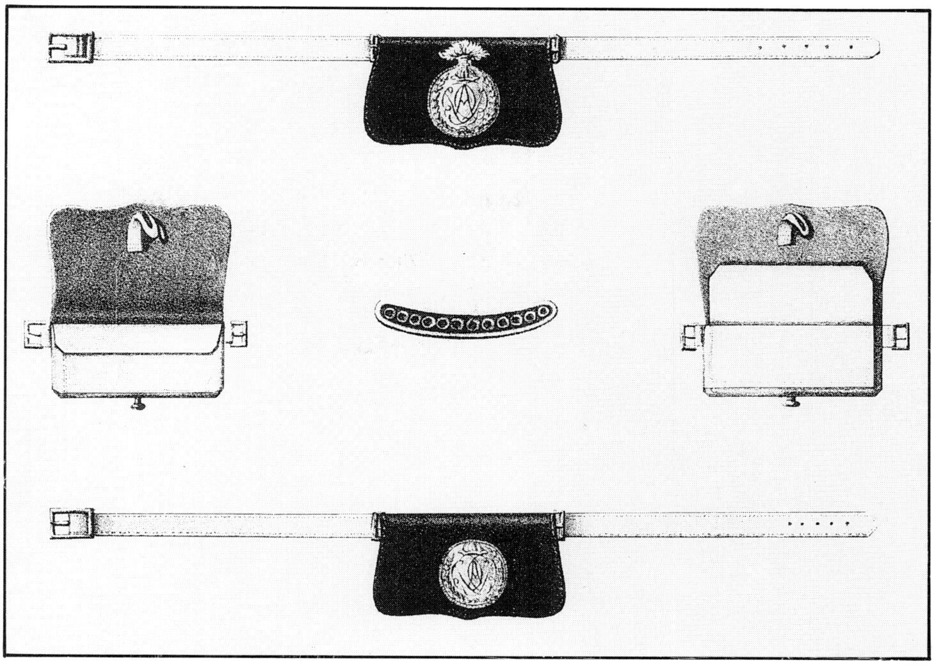

*Grenadier's fuse box (lyandunka), 1700–32, worn in addition to the issued cartridge pouch. The lower example was the type issued to Horse Grenadier regiments. Both are decorated with Peter I's cypher. Engraving from Viskovatov's* Rossiskoi Imperatorskoi Armii *(St. Petersburg 1844–56).*

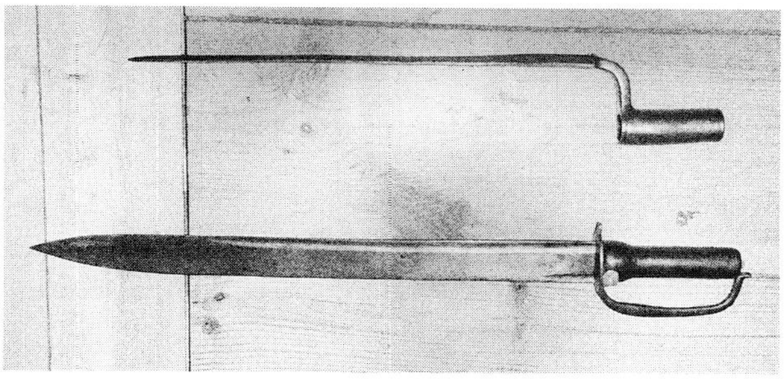

*Russian bayonets, 1700–25. The lower example is a plug bayonet, superseded by the socket bayonet depicted above. (Originals in the State Historic Museum, Moscow)*

The exceptions to the regulation patterns of flags were those of the Guards regiments. Both the Preobrazhenski and Semenovski carried white colonel's colours, while the company colours of the Preobrazhenski were black, and those of the Semenovski light blue. The initial flags of these regiments were lost at Narva, so new standards were issued in 1701. These followed a similar basic pattern to the standards issued to Line regiments but were more ornate, mostly having the common feature of a cross in the top staff corner within a cloud. All used the motif of a gold chain with a St. Andrew's Cross suspended from it. Various devices were used within the chain including the cloud, hand and sword motif of the Line regiments, a Russian eagle and a sailing ship. On some standards the chain was in turn surmounted by either a crown or the 'eye of God' surrounded by a cloud. These standards also carried the crossed palm fronds found on the Line flags.

# THE PLATES

### *A: Voronezh, 1696*

This town on the upper Don served as a springboard for the Russian campaign against Azov in 1696. The army advanced down the Don, supported by a river flotilla, and captured the Turkish fortress after a month-long siege.

### *A1: Streltsi, First Moskva Regiment*

A force of Moscow Streltsi formed part of the Russian army during both Azov campaigns, where their performance was lacklustre. Each regiment was distinguished by a combination of distinctive coat colours and trim. His armament consists of a matchlock musket, a 'Polish' *shashka* and a bardishe (originals in the Kremlin armoury).

### *A2: Soldatski, Lefort's Regiment*

Two 'foreign' regiments participated in the Azov campaign: Gordon's (Butyrski) and Lefort's. The *soldatski's* uniform reflects a combination of Russian and European military fashion, his boots and hat being typically Russian features common during the 17th century. His matchlock musket and sabre are similar to those worn by the Streltsi, and were produced in the workshops of the Kremlin.

*Guard Grenadier of the Preobrazhenski Guard regiment, 1700–25. The representation is based on surviving objects from Russian collections. The grenadier is shown fuzing his grenade. Watercolour by Dmitry Kardovsky, 1909. (Russian Historic Museum, St. Petersburg)*

### *A3: Ukrainian Cossack*

Peter's army included 20,000 Ukrainian and Don Cossacks, who fought with distinction at Azov. Their dress reflected their independent lifestyle. This Zaporozhne carries inlaid firearms, including a 'snaphaunce' musket and a typical Cossack curved *shashka* (originals in the Kremlin Armoury).

### *B: Narva, 1700*

When the Swedes defeated the Russians at Narva, a small knot of troops stood firm. The Guards and two Line regiments defended a wagon laager and fought on until nightfall, so preventing the wholesale slaughter of the Russian troops.

### *B1: Fusilier, Semenovski Guard Regiment*

This Semenovski Guardsman wears the new 'Western' style uniform adopted in 1699, covered by his greatcoat. The musket is a Russian piece, fitted with a 'Baltic-lock' (original in the State Historic Museum). He carries the newly introduced plug bayonet in place of a sword suspended from a leather belt hanger. His 1700–20 pattern of uniform is identifiable by its scalloped pocket flaps.

### *B2: Drummer, Preobrazhenski Guard Regiment*

The uniform of the Petrine drummer differs from that of other troops by the piping on the uniform and the 'swallow's-nest' on his right shoulder, both in the national colours. The drum is suspended from his belt by means of a hook, which could be readjusted to carry the drum over the shoulder when marching. Every infantry regiment included 16 drummers.

### *B3: Pikeman, Preobrazhenski Guard Regiment*

The uniform colours of the Preobrazhenski were adopted by the whole army in 1720. This soldier's pike is adorned with the ceremonial pennon issued to the Guard regiments, although probably not normally carried in action. In addition to his pike and sword he carries a flintlock pistol, as laid down in Golovin's *Artikuly*.

### *C: Dorpat, 1700*

Peter I sought to protect St. Petersburg in 1704 by invading Swedish Livonia. Personally directing the siege of Dorpat, he captured it in July after a five-week bombardment. Narva surrendered in August, so avenging the defeat of 1700.

### *C1: Fusilier, Butyrski Regiment*

This regiment was one of the oldest in the army, and was assigned to the Sheremetev's command in 1704. The Fusilier wears a *kartuz*, which was normally worn turned up. By 1704 the cartridge box carried the Tsar's cypher. He carries a 'dog-lock' musketoon, for which bayonets were never issued (original in Artillery Museum, St. Petersburg).

### *C2: Sergeant, Ingermanlandski Regiment*

This regiment, raised by Alexander Menshikov, was one of the largest and most successful in the army. The sergeant's rank is indicated by the white trim on his coat cuffs and by his sergeant's halberd. A more highly decorated halberd was issued to Guard sergeants.

### *C3: Fusilier, Pskovski Regiment*

One of the most experienced Russian units, this regiment fought at Dorpat, Kalitz, Holowczyn and Poltava. The soldier wears the 1699 pattern of coat with its distinctive scalloped pocket flaps. His armament consists of a Russian copy of a foreign 'fusil' and a plug bayonet (originals in the Kremlin Armoury and State Historic Museum).

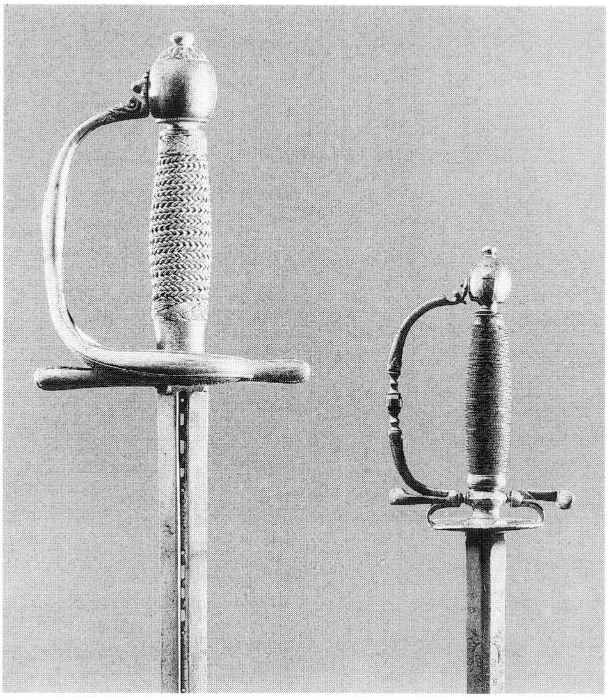

*Russian infantry swords, 1700–25. Although styles differed greatly, the two depicted are fairly representative. The left hand blade is a private's sword, that on the right is an officer's smallsword. (State Museum of the Moscow Kremlin)*

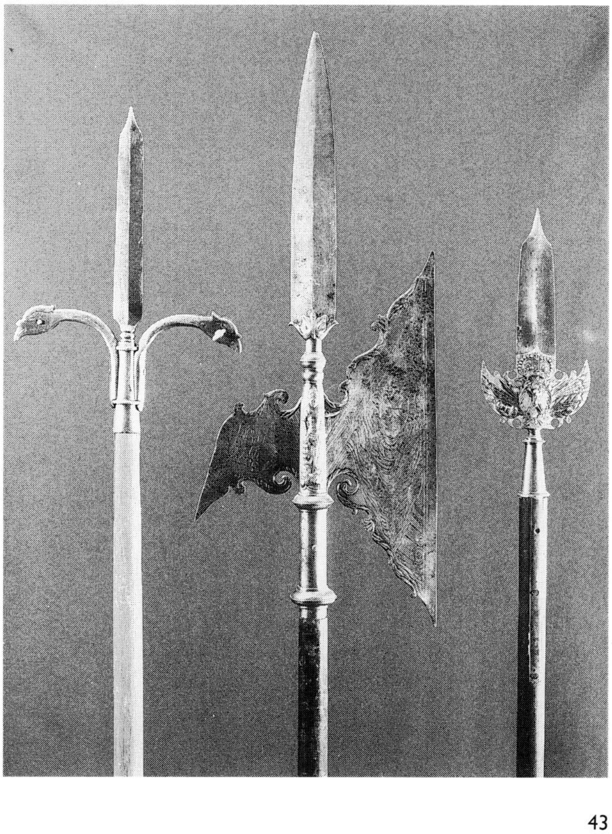

*Russian staff weapons, 1700–25. On the left is a Russian artilleryman's linstock, c.8th. The central weapon is a sergeant's halberd engraved with a Petrine cypher. The officer's partizan on the right is decorated with a crowned St. Andrew's Cross surrounded by a wreath of victory. (State Museums of the Moscow Kremlin)*

### *D: Poltava, 1709*

Charles XII began his 1709 campaign by besieging Poltava, hoping to draw the Russians into battle. Peter's army advanced, then fought a defensive battle, completely destroying the Swedes at Poltava and during the subsequent pursuit.

### *D1: Fusilier, Narvski Regiment*

The regiment consisted of three battalions, all understrength after their defeat at Holowczyn the previous year. This Fusilier carries a Russian-produced 'French-lock' musket (original in the State Historic Museum) and a socket bayonet. A number of contemporary illustrations depict soldiers wearing their stockings over their breeches.

### *D2: Praporshchik, Narvski Regiment*

No standard regulations applied to officers' uniforms, so the coat of this *praporshchik* (ensign) is decorated with gold trim, as is his tricorne. His under-officer's rank is further denoted by his sash and gorget. He carries a smallsword of German pattern, the scabbard worn beneath the coat (original in the Kremlin Armoury). The standard is the colonel's colour of the regiment.

### *D3: Line Grenadier, Prince Repnin's Regiment*

This combined Grenadier regiment survived Holowczyn and participated at Poltava. The uniform differed from that of Line Fusiliers, with the mitre replacing the tricorne, a non-standard coat pattern with pinned coat turnbacks being worn, and the addition of a Grenadier's pouch. This Grenadier is depicted carrying a 'dog-lock' fusil (original in the Artillery Museum, St. Petersburg).

### *E: Poltava, 1709*

This plate is loosely based upon the *Battle of Poltava* mosaic composed by Mikhail Lomonsov, one of several commemorative works emphasising Peter I's participation in the battle.

### *E1: Tsar Peter I*

During the battle the tsar maintained overall com-

Right *The Battle of Poltava, 28 June 1709. The plan depicts several stages of the battle, the Swedes starting in the upper left, facing the Russian redoubts. The final phase was fought in the centre right, in front of the Russian fortified camp. Poltava and the Swedish siegeworks are shown in the centre left. (Royal Armouries, HM Tower of London)*

*The Battle of Poltava, 28 June 1709. The Tsar, escorted by a Dragoon regiment, is depicted in the foreground on a hill that reflects contemporary artistic convention rather than battlefield topography. Engraving by Nicolas de Larmeein, after 1725. (The State Hermitage Museum, St. Petersburg)*

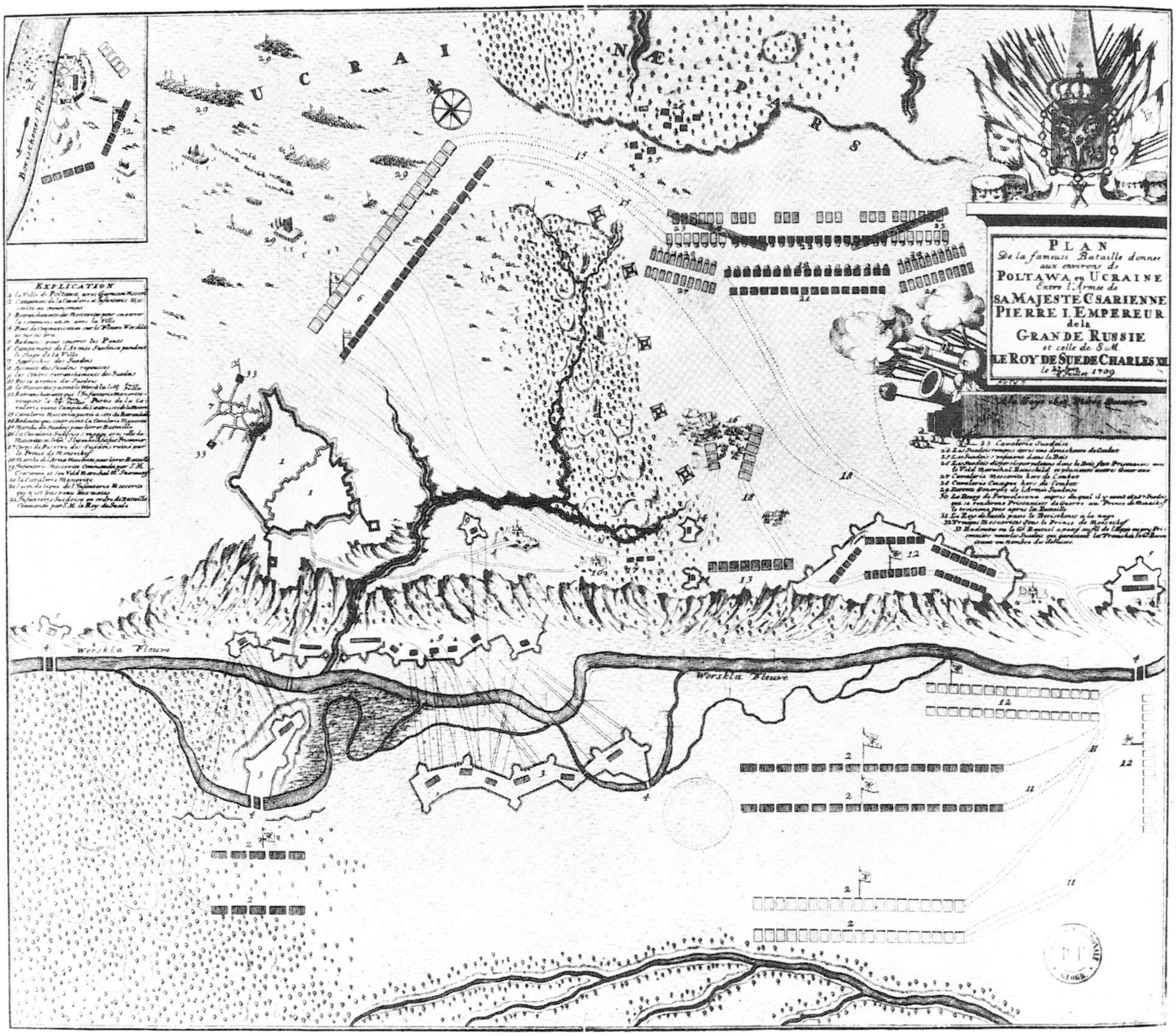


mand of the army, and subsequently led the main infantry body from their entrenchments to meet the Swedish foot. He is reputed to have participated in the action alongside the Preobrazhenski Guard, accompanied by his escorting cavalry squadron. This figure combines the portrayals of the tsar in the Lomonsov mosaic and the painting by Larmessin. The uniform is based upon the original in the State Historic Museum. He wears the sash and cross of the Order of St. Andrew over his uniform coat.

### *E2: Grenadier, Preobrazhenski Guard Regiment*

These élite troops of the Petrine army were armed in a similar manner to Line Grenadiers, carrying a 'fusil', bayonet, smallsword and grenades (originals in the State Historic Museum). The 'fusil' carried is a 'French-lock' weapon produced at Tula. The Grenadier wears a distinctive helmet mitre, adorned with an ostrich feather plume. His coat resembles that issued to Line Grenadiers, with pinned turnbacks. He also carries a Guard cartridge box and his Grenadier box, embellished with the monogram of Peter I. There is no evidence to confirm the legend that the Guard regiments wore grey coats at Poltava in order to deceive the enemy.

### *F: Riga, 1720*

Riga was captured in 1710, completing the Russian conquest of Swedish Livonia. Its defences were

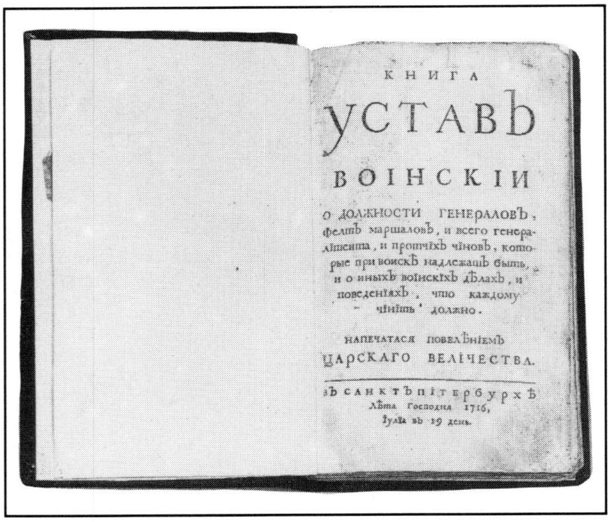
КНИГА
УСТАВЪ
ВОІНСКІИ
о должности генераловъ, фелдъ маршаловъ, и всего генералитета, и прочихъ чиновъ, которые при войскѣ надлежатъ быть, и о иныхъ воинскихъ дѣлахъ, и поведеніяхъ, что каждому чинить должно.
Напечатася повелѣніемъ
царскаго величества.
Въ Санктъпітербурхѣ
лѣта Господня 1716,
іуліа въ 19 день.

*The Military Code of 1716 (*Ustov Voinskoi 1716 goda*). The result of experience gained during the war, the work contained sections on military regulations, tactics and drill. (The Lenin Library, Moscow)*

rebuilt, and the occupying troops were eventually replaced by four garrison regiments.

### *F1: Sergeant, Riga Garrison Regiment*

The regiment was formed in 1712 from soldiers drawn from existing Line regiments. The *seryant* wears a garrison coat cut to the 1720 pattern and trimmed with white braid to denote his rank. He also wears the new pattern of greatcoat. His halberd is a simplified version of that previously issued to the field army (original in the Kremlin Armoury).

### *F2: Fusilier, Ukrainian Land Militia*

Formed in 1713, ostensibly to guard the Ukrainian border, these part-time troops had their origins in a pre-Petrine militia unit. The Fusilier depicted wears an old pattern of coat, and the rest of his equipment reflects the second-line role of his regiment. His headgear is civilian, although tricornes were worn. The militia never saw active service, but were rather used as additional garrison troops.

### *F3: Fusilier, Nekludovski Garrison Regiment*

Unlike the majority of Garrison units this regiment was pre-Petrine, and saw action at Poltava. He wears the collarless working coat issued to Garrison troops, a coarser version of the army *kaftan*. His fusil is of an obsolete pattern. The relative safety of garrison life was balanced by low pay and frequent manual labour.

### *G: Derbent, 1722*

Taking advantage of internal strife in the Persian Empire, Peter invaded the area between the Georgian and Caspian Seas. In a two-year campaign he pacified the region, now modern Daghestan, Georgia and Azerbaijan.

### *G1: Grenadier, Kampenhausen's Regiment*

The uniform is almost identical to that of D3, but features a coat cut in the 1720 pattern. The new uniforms followed the colours adopted by the Preobrazhenski Guards. His 'French-lock' fusil was produced at Olonetz (original in the Kremlin Armoury). Grenadiers from this regiment were detailed to provide troops for the new *Nizevoi Dorpous* regiments.

### *G2: Fusilier, St. Petersbourgski Regiment*

He wears the 1720 pattern coat with its wide collar, and simplified pocket flap for both coat and vest. The dark green coat colour became the standard for all infantry regiments from 1720 until the late 19th century. His 'fusil' and sword are both of Russian manufacture (originals in the Kremlin Armoury). The regiment was initially raised by the Governor of St. Petersburg for the defence of the city.

### *G3: Major, Simbirski Regiment*

This over-officer wears his own version of the 1720 pattern soldier's coat, embellished with braid. Note the brass gorget worn under the collar but over the silken necktie. Other badges of rank include his sash in a variation of the national colours, and a partizan. Both sword and partizan were produced in Tula (originals in the State Historic Museum and Kremlin Armoury respectively).

### *H: Colours*

### *H1: Colonel's colour, Preobrazhenski Guard Regiment, c.1701*

This colour replaced the standard lost at Narva, and was carried throughout the Great Northern War. Its predecessor depicted a brown Russian eagle on a white field. (Source: Viskovatov)

*Fusilier of a Line regiment, 1720–32. Note the simpler cut of the coat pockets compared with the pre-1720 uniform. He is depicted firing a Russian-produced 'fusil'. Engraving from Viskovatov's* Rossiskoi Imperatorskoi Armii *(St. Petersburg, 1844–56).*

***H2: Company colour, Preobrazhenski Guard Regiment, c.1706***
One of several post-1700 designs used on company colours. All standards had a black field. Others resembled the colonel's colour without the outer foliage, and with the 'eye of God' within a cloud replacing the crown. (Source: Viskovatov)

***H2: Colonel's colour, Semenovski Guard Regiment, c.1701***
This resembles the Preobrazhenski colour without the foliage denoting the premier regiment. Later colonel's colours replaced the crown with an 'eye of God' as in H4. (Source: Viskovatov)

***H4: Company colour, Semenovski Guard Regiment, c.1706***
One of two designs used by the regiment, the other replacing the 'eye of God' with a gold crown. The two stars denote that it belongs to the third company; the first (or senior) company colour was unadorned. (Source: Viskovatov)

***H5: Colour, Line Regiments, 1700–12***
This standard, with slight variations, was used for both the colonel's and company colours for all Line and Grenadier regiments. Company colours had a coloured field and used the system of stars depicted in H4. (Source: Viskovatov)

***H6: Colonel's colour, Line Regiments, 1712–25***
This design was issued to all Line and Grenadier regiments, replacing H5. The company colours (not illustrated) combined a geometric design with a regional motif in the upper staff corner. (Source: Viscovatov)

## Notes sur les planches en couleur

A1 Les couleurs caractéristiques du manteau et ses bordures identifient chaque régiment dans la force de Moscou Streltsi qui se bat, sans grand crédit, dans les campagnes d'Azov. Les armes sont un sabre de style polonais, un mousquet à mèche et une bardische – ce dernier sert come arme ainsi que pose-mousquet. **A2** Soldat du vieux régiment 'étranger' portant des habits qui illustrent les influences russes (les bottes et le chapeau) ainsi que les influences de l'ouest. Le mousquet à mèche et la sabre sont fabriqués dans l'arsenal du Kremlin. **A3** L'habit caractéristique des Cossacks Zaporozhne est tout à fait irrégulier; à noter le mousquet incrusté 'snaphaunce' et le sabre Cossack 'shashka'.

B1 Le nouvel uniforme de 1699/1700 du style de l'ouest est porté sous le manteau; les revers des poches sont à festons. Son mousquet Baltique fabriqué en Russie porte la nouvelle baïonnette à tampon et s'attache à sa ceinture à la place de l'épée. **B2** Le passepoil et la décoration en 'nid d'hirondelle' sur son épaule identifient l'uniforme du joueur de tambour. **B3** Les couleurs régimentales de cette unité élite seront plus tard adoptées par tous les uniformes de l'infantrie. La pique porte ici les banderoles cérémonial des Gardes mais n'est probablement pas portée pendant la bataille. Les porteurs de piques sont armés d'une épée et d'un pistolet à pierre.

C1 A noter la casquette 'kartuz', la boîte à cartouches portant le monogramme du Tsar et le mousqueton à chien sans baïonnette. **C2** Le rang est indiqué par la bordure blanches sur les manchettes et la hallebarde. **C3** Manteau de motif 1699/1700 avec les poches à festons; 'Fusil' importé avec baïonnette à tampon.

D1 Les peintures de l'époque illustrent parfois les bas qui sont tirés par dessus les haut-de-chausses. L'arme est un fusil mousquet russe avec une baïonnette à douille. **D2** Aucune régulation stricte ne gouverne l'uniforme des officiers; cette insigne a une bordure de dentelle dorée. Son rang de 'sous officier' est indiqué par son écharpe et son gorget. Il porte l'épée de chevet de style allemand. Le drapeau est de la couleur de colonel du régiment. **D3** Membre d'un régiment de Grenadiers combiné, il porte la coiffe charactéristique, le manteau non-régulier et l'étui des Grenadiers.

E1 A pour source un uniforme d'époque qui survit et les illustrations de Pierre dans la peinture de Larmessin et la mosaïque de Lomonsov. **E2** Cette unité élite se distingue des Grenadiers de Ligne par la coiffe, et par les détails de sa cartouche et de l'étui des grenadiers.

F1 Manteau du modèle 1720 de l'infantrie de garnison avec le galon de rang blanc puis le manteau du nouveau style; la hallebarde est d'un motif simplifié. **F2** L'uniforme de l'ancien style et le matériel rappellent le rôle secondaire de cette armée; la coiffe est civile. **F3** En contraste avec les autres régiments de Garnison, cette unité a vu l'action at Poltava. Il porte le manteau de travail sans col qui est caractéristique des unités de Garnison et il pote un fusil désuet.

G1 Quasiment identique à D3, et noter que ceci est le modèle 1720 de l'uniforme dans les couleurs qu'on a adoptées des Gardes Preobrazhenski; il porte un fusil mousquet. **G2** Le manteau de 1720 a un col plus large et les revers des poches simplifiés. **G3** Le Commandant porte sa version personnelle du manteau du soldat qui date de 1720 avec les galons ajoutés et le gorget en cuivre. Son écharpe et la pertuisanne sont des marques du rang de l'officier (la pertuisanne est plutôt par les sous-officiers que par les officiers supérieurs) mais les armes portés sont d'un choix personnel.

H1 Ceci a remplacé le drapeau porté à Narva, et est utilisé pendant le reste de la Grande Guerre du Nord. **H2** Un modèle parmi plusieurs motifs des couleurs qui datent d'après 1700; les autres ressemblent au drapeau du colonel mais avec 'l'oeil de Dieu' qui remplace la courronne et sans le feuillage extérieur. **H3** Ressemble au drapeau H1 mais sans le feuillage qui signifie le premier rang de Preobrazhenski. **H4** Un des deux motifs utilisés par le régiment, l'autre qui remplace 'l'oeil de Dieu' avec une courronne dorée. Les deux étoiles identifient la 3ème Compagnie – le drapeau de la 1ère Compagnie ne porte pas d'étoiles. **H5** Avec de petites variations, on utilise ce motif pour les drapeaux du colonel ainsi que les drapeaux des compagnies et ceci dans tous les régiments de Ligne et de Grenadier. Les drapeaux des Compagnies ont les champs de couleur et le système d'étoiles figuré en H4. **H6** A remplacé H5 pour toutes les couleurs des colonels, dans les régiments de Ligne et de Grenadier à partir de 1712.

## Farbtafeln

A1 Verschiedene Mantelfarben und Besätze identifizierten die einzelnen Regimenter der Moskauer Streltzi, die – ohne sich besonders auszuzeichnen – in den asowschen Feldzügen mitkämpften. Bei den Waffen handelt es sich um einen Säbel polnischen Stils, eine Luntenschloßmuskete und eine "Bardische", sowohl als Waffe wie als Musketenauflage dienend. **A2** Soldat des alten Fremden-Regiments in einer Kleidung, die sowohl russische (Stiefel, Hut) wie westliche Einflüsse zeigt. Luntenmuskete und Säbel stammen aus den Waffenkammern des Kreml. **A3** Typische Kleidung der Zaporozhne-Kosaken, sehr irregulär; siehe eingelegte Schnappschloßmuskete und Kosakensäbel.

B1 Die neue Uniform nach westlicher Art von 1699–1700 wird unter dem langen Mantel getragen; sie hat bogenförmige Taschen. Seine in Rußland hergestellte Muskete mit "baltischem" Schloß hat das neue Aufsteck-Bajonett, das anstelle eines Schwerts an seinem Gürtel hängt. **B2** Paspel und "Schwalbennest"-Schulterverzierung kennzeichen die Trommler-Uniform. **B3** Die Regimentsfarben dieser Elite-Einheit wurden später für alle Infanterie-Uniformen angenommen. Die Pike ist hier mit der zeremoniellen Standarte der Garde versehen, die wahrscheinlich nicht in der Schlacht getragen wurde. Pikeniere trugen ein Schwert und eine Steinschloßpistole.

C1 Siehe Kártuz-Kappe, Patronentasche mit zaristischem Abzeichen und "Hundsschloß"-Muiskete ohne Bajonett. **C2** Rang wird durch weiße Manschetten-Aufschläge und die Hellebarde angezeigt. **C3** Mantel im Stil von 1699–1770 mit bogenförmigen Taschen und importierte Steinschloßmuskete mit Aufsteck-Bajonett.

D1 In zeitgendössischen Abbildungen sieht man gelegentlich die Strümpfe über die Breeches gezogen. Er trägt eine russische Muskete mit "Franzosenschloß" und Steckbajonett. **D2** Offiziersuniformen wurden nicht durch strenge Bestimmungen reguliert; dieser Fähnrich zeigt Goldlitzenbesatz. Sein "Unter-Offiziers"-Status wird durch die Schärpe und die Halsberge angezeigt, und er trägt ein Kurzschwert nach deutschem Stil. Die Flagge ist die des Regiments-Obristen. **D3** Angehöriger eines kombinierten Grenadierregiments mit typischer Kopfbedeckung, unüblichem Mantel und Grenadiertasche.

E1 Beruhend auf erhaltener Uniform und auf Abbildungen von Peter in dem Gemälde von Larmessin und dem Mosaik von Lomonsow. **E2** Diese Elite-Einheit unterscheidet sich von den Liniengrenadieren durch die Kopfbedeckung und durch Details der Patronen- und Grenadiertaschen.

F1 Rock der Garnisonsinfanterie mit weißen Rang-Litzen und Mantel neuen Stils; Hellebarde in vereinfachtem Stil. **F2** Die Uniform nach altem Stil und die Ausrüstung zeigen die zweitklassige Rolle dieser Miliz; siehe zivilistische Kopfbedeckung. **F3** Im Gegensatz zu den meisten Garnisonsregimentern war diese Einheit bei Poltava im Einsatz. Er trägt die für Garnisonstruppen typische kragenlose Arbeitsjacke und eine altmodische Muskete.

G1 Bei einem Vergleich mit der beinahe identischen Uniform in D3 kann man feststellen, daß dies die Uniform in Stil von 1720 ist, mit den Farben, die nach denen der Preobrazhenski-Garden angenommen wurden; er trägt eine französisch aussehende Steinschloßmuskete. **G2** Dr Mantel von 1720 hatte einen breiteren Kragen und vereinfachte Taschenklappen **G3** Ein major mit seiner eigenen Version des Soldatenrocks von 1720 mit zusätzlichen Litzen und Messing-Halsberge. Seine Schärpe und Hellebarde zeigen den Offizierstrang an; die Hellebarde war eher das Zeichen eins "Unter-Offiziers", doch Waffen wurden nach persönlicher Wahl getragen.

H1 Diese Flagge ersetzte jene, die bei Narva und im Rest des großen Nordischen Krieges getragen wurde. **H2** Eines von mehreren Kompaniefahnen-Mustern nach 1700; andere glichen der Obristen-Fahne, aber mit dem "Auge Gottes" anstatt der Krone, und ohne das äußere Laubwerk. **H3** Ähnlich wie H1, aber ohne das Laubwerk, das den Vorrang der Preobrazhenski-Garden markierte. **H4** Eines von zwei von diesem Regiment verwendeten Mustern; bei dem anderen wurde das "Auge Gottes" von einer goldenen Krone ersetzt. Die beiden Sterne kennzeichnen die 3. Kompanie – die Flagge der 1. Kompanie trug keine Sterne. **H5** Dieses Muster wurde mit kleinen Variationen sowohl für die Obristen- wie für die Kompanieflaggen aller Linien- und Grenadierregimenter verwendet. Kompaniefahnen hatten farbige Felder und das Sternensystem, das in H4 zu sehen ist. **H6** Dadurch wurde ab 1712 H5 als Obritenflagge bei allen Linien- und Garderegimentern ersetzt.